THE
POLITICS
OF
DEFEAT

THE
POLITICS
OF
DEFEAT

*America's Decline
in the
Middle East*

BY JOSEPH CHURBA

CYRCO PRESS, INC., PUBLISHERS • NEW YORK AND LONDON

Source of maps:
Central Intelligence Agency
August 1976
Superintendent of Documents, U.S. Gov't Printing Office
Stock Number 041-015-00080-2

Manufactured in the United States of America

First Printing

DISTRIBUTED BY THE BOBBS-MERRILL CO., INC.,
INDIANAPOLIS, INDIANA

FOR MY FATHER

CONTENTS

FOREWORD

BECAUSE of Dr. Churba's intimate familiarity with the constantly shifting hotbed of Byzantine politics in the strategically vital Near and Middle East, he has unquestionably emerged as one of the foremost American experts on the pressing problems of that region and on superpower rivalry there. His politically realistic analyses have provoked storms in Washington that culminated in his forced resignation as senior Middle East intelligence analyst for the Air Force.

What is fascinating and at the same time disturbing to read in Dr. Churba's book is the extent to which the power hierarchy in Washington is paralyzed in its efforts to perceive the true American national interest in the Middle East. Basking in a dream world of political un-

9

reality, arising largely from preconceived notions that are reinforced by special interests, this power hierarchy has fostered policies that have proved to be counterproductive to the United States. As a result, it has contributed to the erosion of our national strategic interest in the region, with implications that are virtually global.

Dr. Churba argues that this lamentable trend can still, perhaps, be reversed. To roll back Soviet influence, one priority of United States foreign policy must be reoriented to forge and sustain a solid alliance with Turkey, Israel and Iran.

—George Schwab
City University of New York
May, 1977

INTRODUCTION

IN this book, Joseph Churba performs a service of high value for his country and for all students of strategy, history and Middle Eastern affairs in general. Free of the analytic myopia which characterizes many current commentators on the subject. Dr. Churba compels his readers to view developments in the Middle East as a collective component of larger issues, including inter-state relations in neighboring regions and the over-arching strategic relationship between the United States and the Soviet Union. Though Dr. Churba's views and my own do not mesh on all issues, I find his book bright, stimulating, and generally reflective of strategic realities as I know them.

The tendency to portray the Arab-Israeli conflict simply

as a regional affair, divorced from military developments in South Asia, Southern Europe and Africa, has been evident in the diplomacy of recent United States administrations. To some extent we can attribute this lack of scope to the mental squint which many administration analysts develop after years of specialization, but a more enlightening explanation can be found in the Nixon-Kissinger conception of detente.

Few foreign policies ever received such hucksterish promotion. Few foreign policies ever exacted such a price from the American people, and few foreign policies ever failed so abjectly. Detente between the superpowers was touted as a foundation for a "lasting structure of international peace." Its pursuit, it was clear, would entail a high cost in the form of wheat, manufactured goods, and advanced technology; but compensation was to be found in the restraints which it would impose on aggressive Soviet behavior. The Nixon administration, however, grappling as it was with a monstrous domestic scandal, believed it necessary to hitch its political future to the apparent success of its detente policy—even as that domestic scandal was enticing the Soviets to employ detente as a cloak to cover a series of Soviet transgressions. Having committed itself irreversibly to detente, the administration lost the diplomatic leverage necessary to constrain the Kremlin's foreign adventures. This loss was confirmed in October 1973, when Moscow coordinated with Egypt and Syria in contemptuous violation of a four-month-old United States-Soviet accord, but pursuant to an established plan which antedated that accord: a sneak attack against the state of Israel. Obtrusive Soviet intervention on behalf of the Arab war effort, and publicized Soviet pledges of military protection for participants in the oil embargo, exposed the fact that the Nixon administration's political life preserver, detente, had sprung a leak. In an effort to patch up the damage, the secretary of state advanced the lame assertion that without his detente policy the Soviets would have acted worse. Despite clear evidence to the contrary, Dr. Kissinger proclaimed detente healthy. In doing so, he implicitly established the principle that Soviet aggression in the Middle East—and, it would appear to follow, in other "peripheral" parts of the world—has no significant impact on basic relations between the superpowers. This decoupling of "local" events from the broad strategic scheme of things has served to mislead the American public as to the actual ramifications of regional developments around the globe—a result which Dr. Kissinger himself was forced to lament during the Angolan crisis. It has also served to cloud popular understanding of the nature and extent of Soviet involvement in the Middle East and the long-term motivation underlying this involvement.

Dr. Churba explores in illuminating detail the gamut of Soviet Middle Eastern ambitions. In the course of this exploration, he concentrates incisively on the essential negative goal of Soviet strategists: the power to arrest by force the distribution of Arab oil to the West and its allies. In this petroleum-lubricated era, the rulers of the Soviet Union have discovered an even more compelling reason than had occurred to their expansionist Czarist predecessors for cultivating Russian influence in the Middle East. The modern strategic stakes being what they are, the Soviet Union has chosen to insure the permanence of its Middle Eastern presence by establishing multiple and diverse footholds. Consequently, as we learn from Dr. Churba, Soviet activities in the area range broadly, extending far beyond the mere patronizing of the Arab campaign to eliminate Israel. In fact, inspection reveals the insinuation of the Soviets into virtually every one of the almost countless rivalries and conflicts among the Arab states themselves. Dr. Churba's analysis persuasively and thoroughly belies the common hypothesis that should Israel disappear from the map the Soviets would lose their "excuse" for meddling in the Middle East. Ignorance of the breadth and degree of Soviet involvement in the Arab world has accounted for much that is wrong with America's Middle East policy. It has caused administration officials to undervalue our democratic friends in Israel and to exult excessively over the occasional garnering by the United States of transitory claims on the affections of unstable Arab autocrats. If an excuse ever existed for this ignorance, it has assuredly been voided with the publication of this book.

Rarely does an accounting of the American-Israeli relationship include mention of its military value to the United States. Dr. Churba's work, therefore, fills a gap in our strategic literature by evaluating Israel's role in American military planning. Dr. Churba's conclusions as to the importance of this role rest upon sound and articulated reasoning. They are supported by my own personal experience in dealing with United States strategy in the Middle East. Israel's military value to the United States derives not only from its location adjacent to the oil-rich Persian Gulf region, at the junction of three continents, but also from the sophistication and prodigious efficiency of its defense forces. More important than either of these factors, however, is the reliability of the state of Israel as a comrade-in-arms on behalf of the essential interests of the Western world—interests which inevitably harmonize with those of the Jewish state as a result of the latter's dedication to the principles of democratic government. The record of productive cooperation between Washington and Jerusalem during both the 1970 Jordanian civil war and the recent war in Lebanon attests to this harmony of interests and to its utility to the United States. Israel's deployment of artillery and troops near the battlefronts during these crises spared American leaders the terrible choice of either injecting their own military forces into the region or abandoning to Soviet-supported armies our Jordanian allies or the Lebanese Christians.

Unfortunately, appreciation of Israel's value as a militarily potent ally is not what it should be in certain Pentagon circles. Recent years have witnessed a substantial loss of sympathy among key United States defense officials for arms requests from Jerusalem. The reluctance of these officials to release military hardware to the Israelis stems in part from the concern that the equipment will be difficult to replace quickly. Recent cuts in the United States defense budget have intensified this concern. However, given the efficient use to which Israel puts the military goods it receives, it is a dangerous mistake automatically to exalt service readiness over alliance readiness. Were its defense budget adequate, the United States could generate sufficient military stocks to obviate any need for "rationing" essential arms among its allies and itself.

It must also be noted that general Pentagon esteem

for Israel diminished in proportion to the "success" of
Dr. Kissinger's Middle East diplomacy. In the view of
some United States defense analysts, Israel's unilateral
withdrawals from militarily valuable territory, unaccom-
panied as they were by Arab concessions of commensurate
value, reduced, justifiably or not, the apparent usefulness
of American-Israeli military cooperation. According to
these analysts, these withdrawals weakened Israel's strategic posture in the region and thus lessened, at least
marginally, its military value to the United States. Furthermore, the withdrawals registered in many minds as evidence that Israel's steadfastness under pressure could no
longer be assumed with certainty. Israel can ill afford to
lose its reputation for pluckiness.

It need hardly be pointed out that the administration
in Washington is in a unique position to relieve the strain
on Israel's reputation and integrity. Dr. Churba argues
forcefully for such relief. I agree. The United States can
ill afford to lose Israel.

—Admiral Elmo R. Zumwalt, Jr.
Chief of Naval Operations, U.S.N., Ret.

PREFACE

THE purpose of this book is simple. It is to demonstrate that the vitality of Israel is crucial to the United States and that the United States must therefore categorically commit itself to the defense and preservation of that nation. We must not support Israel merely because there are millions of Jews in this country whose electoral backing would otherwise be lost. We must not support her merely because she embodies the last, determined stand of a people persecuted through the centuries and because our commitment to the principles of humanity, decency and sovereignty warrant nothing less. We must support Israel primarily because she is—and will remain—of paramount strategic value to the security of the United States.

We must also make our support known. We cannot simply demand peace. Peace may not be in the offing. Reason does not appear to inspire some of the parties involved. We cannot say that there is more than one side to this question, and that they all deserve to be heard. There are many sides. Some may deserve to be heard. Some also may not. What is clear is that we must take a stand, and that this stand should be based on where our interests lie. Our interests, as this book will attempt to show, lie first with Israel.

Yet that is not what our foreign policy has reflected. Driven by the belief that an alignment with Arab nationalism is necessary for the security of the United States, high American officials have continued to denigrate the importance of Israel as a concrete and reliable asset in our broader strategic equation. This, despite the fact that Israel has grown stronger, not weaker, through the years— so much stronger, in fact, that the cost-benefit ratio of our military support for Israel is higher than that for any of our other allies except perhaps the Federal Republic of Germany.

It is now a matter of public record that obstruction to Jewish statehood originated among high officials within the State Department, when in 1948 they ignored direct presidential orders to support the partition of Palestine and the creation of a Jewish state.* What was essentially a political decision, made by President Truman in the long-term interests of the American people, was opposed by misguided bureaucrats in the naive belief that Israel would be a Soviet stooge and that the Arabs could be manipulated into an alliance against the Soviet Union.

---

* Read Clark M. Clifford, "Factors Influencing President Truman's Decision to Support Partition and Recognize the State of Israel," presented to the American Jewish Historical Society and the American Historical Association, Washington, D.C., 23 December 1976.

The State Department officials concerned had to fulfill a responsibility in this matter to the president or otherwise resign. They did neither. Instead, they moved to support a United Nations Trusteeship Proposal for Palestine which would have nullified the partition plan—thereby aborting the creation of Israel. Without President Truman's courage and leadership, this country would have shown no support for Jewish statehood.

This attitude continues in Washington officialdom. Symbolic of it is the State Department's refusal to recognize Jerusalem as the capital of the Jewish state. Israel is the only nation where the United States embassy is not located in its capital. Our refusal to rectify this anomaly serves only to strengthen the Arab claim that there is an inherent deficiency in Israel's national sovereignty. To date, no American president has succeeded in loosening the formidable grip on United States Middle Eastern policy of the anti-Israel forces in the State Department.

Similar attitudes prevail at the Pentagon. When, in 1974,* General George S. Brown, Chairman of the Joint Chiefs of Staff, made inaccurate and disparaging public remarks about American Jews and their relationship to United States support for Israel, President Ford reprimanded him. When he characterized Israel as a military "burden" during an interview published in October of 1976, he provoked sharp rejoinders from several quarters.†

* *The Washington Post*, 13 November 1974.
† Including this writer. My disagreement with General Brown was reported in *The New York Times* on 20 October 1976. At the time, I was a Special Advisor to Air Force Intelligence at the Pentagon and the Air Force's senior Middle East intelligence estimator. The Pentagon's reaction to my comments was to suspend my special security clearances. I was told I had "technically violated" Defense Department regulations,

Aside from invading the civilian policy-making arena, General Brown had in fact said precisely what the Soviets and the Arabs have been telling the world in order to advance their own global strategic designs. In lending his high office to the Soviet-Arab stratagem of isolating the United States from Israel, General Brown sent the wrong signals to Moscow and the Arab capitals. He thereby increased uncertainty as to whether the United States would respond in the event of renewed hostilities in the Middle East.

It is clear that our policies in the Middle East are under the sway of an inexorable defeatism. The Brown episode is only the exposed tip of that policy, which has extended over many decades. It is the purpose of this book to highlight the dangers inherent in the defeatist idea that Israel constitutes a "burden."

While the United States functions in the Middle East from a perspective which trades long-term strategic interests for transitory gain, Israel attempts to execute a "Policy for Survival." We tend to forget Israel is the only country threatened with extinction. As a modern independent nation, Israel has both the will and the means to exercise its sovereignty. It will meet any challenges to its security, even if it must meet them alone. An American policy which forgets this fact at a time of increasing Soviet aggression further runs the risk of defeat.

A review of our policy in the Middle East suggests, indeed, that the trauma of our experience in Southeast Asia has had a profound impact on our ability to deal

---

though it was never explained how. Because the suspension of clearances made it impossible for me to discharge my official duties, it forced my resignation.

with questions of national security. It is as though there were now a subconscious desire in the American psyche to salvage our sense of national worth by not taking initiatives from positions of strength. We seem obsessed with the fear of another failure.

We miscalculated the indigenous forces in Vietnam. Are we now subconsciously seeking to apply that lesson to areas where it does not pertain? Have we lost our ability to relate to other totally different regions of the world in terms that meet their own special realities?

Paradoxically, when it comes to asserting American power, the only country our policymakers can find to abuse is Israel. Future historians may ask whether the Kissingerian browbeating of Israel in 1975 as "intransigent" was an attempt to assuage the moral wounds of Vietnam by asserting American "manhood" over Israel—our only successful military asset in the Middle East.

Any further faltering by the United States with regard to our moral and strategic commitments to Israel would shake our sense of inner worth as a nation. It would also shake the faith of our staunchest allies. Most countries, be they allies or friends of expediency, see nothing but hyprocrisy in our continued placation of the Arab oil Sheikhs.

In such circumstances, the Soviet Union is certain more doggedly to test our will and resolve in the world arena. Ambiguity and indecision can lead only to disastrous results, whether we finally oppose Soviet aggression or not. It will be no comfort to America to have proved that the Soviets had miscalculated.

And what if the Soviets have not miscalculated? The present course of United States policy will enable the

Soviets to achieve dominance in the Middle East and global strategic superiority over America. Under such circumstances, it would be criminal for anyone to suggest denying the Kremlin its *Pax Sovietica* at the risk—for it would then be the only other option available—of nuclear conflagration.

Washington, D. C.
May, 1977

ACKNOWLEDGMENTS

A growing segment of the articulate public is becoming
ever more disenchanted with our foreign policy.
The arena of the Middle East is but one example. Our
occasional foreign policy triumphs there are always overshadowed by our defeats. This book is an analysis of
why that is so, and it examines the role played by our
foreign policy establishment in contributing to the erosion of our influence in this strategically vital area.

To acknowledge everyone with whom I have discussed
and argued different points is impossible. Nevertheless,
I wish to express my gratitude first and foremost to
Mr. Aaron David Rosenbaum, Director of Research for
the American-Israel Public Affairs Committee, as well
as to the following: Professor Gil Carl AlRoy of the

City University of New York, Mr. Everett J. Burlando, the Honorable Eugene P. Foley, President of the National Committee on American Foreign Policy, Inc., Mr. William J. Mazzocco, and Dr. Fred Schulman. Of course, the responsibility for every thought that has finally been included in this book is solely mine.

JOSEPH CHURBA

Washington, D. C.
May, 1977

I

THE STRATEGIC
SIGNIFICANCE
OF THE
MIDDLE EAST

AMERICAN interests in the Middle East are multiple and complex. These include the maintenance of strategic access to the region and of secure access to its oil supplies, the containment of local disputes, continued economic development and social progress, the protection of American investment and of its contribution to the United States balance of payments, furtherance of American trade, and the preservation and expansion of cultural ties with the peoples of the region.

America's paramount interest in the Middle East, however, is politico-strategic: to prevent the area from falling under the domination of the Soviet Union and being manipulated against the West. Were Moscow allowed to establish its dominance or acquire a stranglehold on the jugular of Persian Gulf oil, the capacity of both NATO and Japan to resist Soviet pressure would be drastically impaired. Iran and Turkey would be effectively neutralized.

Strategically, such a development would lead to the neutralization of Europe, the encirclement of China and the eventual isolation of the United States. To avert this possibility, the United States over the past three decades promoted various regional security arrangements, including the Middle East Command and Defense Organization from 1951 to 1952, the Baghdad Pact in 1955 and CENTO in 1959.* It also concluded bilateral agreements with Turkey, Iran and Pakistan in 1959 and drew Greece and Turkey into NATO in 1952. Principles relative to peace, security and the flow of arms into the Arab-Israeli zone were also embodied in the Tripartite Declaration of May, 1950, but the major response to the growth of Soviet influence in the region lay in the Eisenhower Doctrine of March, 1957.[1] Reflecting and supporting these commitments is the American military presence, notably the Sixth Fleet in the Mediterranean.

In addition to a growing interest in the containment of Soviet power, the United States has two other major concerns in the area. One has to do with the survival of Israel—a matter of vital interest to the general American public, and therefore a political factor of considerable importance. The second relates to private economic interests, principally those of the American oil companies

---

* An acronym for Central Treaty Organization, a defense alliance with which the United States is associated, comprising Great Britain, Iran, Turkey and Pakistan—the remaining countries of the Baghdad Pact after Iraq's withdrawal made the latter name inappropriate.

engaged in the production, refining and marketing of that commodity in world trade. The two priorities often clash, and the exponents of each have argued that their particular interest coincides with the national strategic interest. Suffice it to say at this point that the American oil companies have become the inadvertent agents of Arab oil policy and Arab Middle Eastern policy. Their stance may be justified in terms of private monetary gain, but not in terms of American national strategic interests.

As for the argument that United States support for Israel hampers the development of American investments in and trade with the Arab countries, it has been sufficiently documented that economic considerations normally prevail when mutually beneficial. Even direct American investment in Israel has not deterred the Arabs from doing business with such companies when it has been found beneficial for their economies. An example of this is the selective enforcement of the Arab League's boycott of firms blacklisted because of their relationships with Israel.

Similarly, the allegation that support for Israel constitutes an obstacle to Arab petrodollar investments in the United States, investments which might greatly help alleviate the balance-of-payments deficit, ignores actual Arab behavior. As with OPEC prices, their primary considerations have been economic, which explains why a country like Italy—despite its almost unqualified support of the Arab position—obtains little Arab capital while the United States receives unprecedented Arab investments. Arab political and business leaders have invariably acted in a business-like manner, giving economic considerations the highest priority. Indeed, the issue is not how to induce Arab investment, but how to limit and control it to mutual advantage.

While economic considerations are important, they must not deter us from a clear understanding of vital United States security interests. It is clearly in the interest of United States security to insure Israel's capacity to exercise fully its stabilizing influence in the area. Support for Israel has become a bipartisan American position, endorsed by every administration since 1948. Indeed, in Israel the United States has the only democratic friend in the region whose affinity with the West is not dependent on the survival or caprice of an autocratic ruler.

The paramount rationale for a strategic alignment with Israel is rooted in national necessity. To preserve our institutions and our way of life, the United States requires a global environment in which Western Europe and Japan are reasonably stable, secure and friendly to America, while Africa, Asia and Australia remain independent of the Soviet Union or China. Accordingly, it is necessary that Russia and China remain rivals and that China remain free of an encircling Soviet threat—such as would result from Soviet predominance in the Indian Ocean, the Western Pacific and adjacent land areas. A fully encircled China would no longer effectively check the Soviet Union and so sustain a triangular balance in which the American effort could be small.

Together with the obvious need to avoid a United States-Soviet nuclear confrontation, these are the permanent requirements of United States foreign policy. Of necessity, they must override short-term considerations, and they set the dominant framework for policy. For example, while regional considerations and domestic attitudes incline the United States to sympathize with India, the overriding global requirement is to protect China's southern flank—and this can be done only by ensuring a viable Pakistan, even at the expense of closer ties with India.

In this global framework Israel's role is singular. It arises from the unique characteristics of Israeli society and its special link with the United States. The link is viewed as "organic" regardless of all imaginable political and economic changes that may intervene. And inasmuch as Israel represents the only secure logistical link in the entire region between Western Europe and Japan, its role as an access point makes it indispensable to any solid Western security structure. From this perspective, American support for a strong Israel can be justified wholly on the grounds of "national interest"—grounds valid in all circumstances except in the context of a totally isolationist America.

The periodic explosions in the Arab-Israeli conflict have clouded Israel's role on behalf of American interests. They have led to the conceptual delusion that the removal of the Arab-Israeli issue would lead to a solidly pro-Western Arab world. Few observers of Middle East politics have ever advanced the proposition that the periodic eruptions between Arab countries themselves are equally as chronic as the Arab-Israeli conflict. Assuming that these regional conflicts—among Arabs as well as between them and Israel—will continue to beset the Middle East and encourage Soviet intervention, Israel's role appears in an entirely different light.

Although American support for Israel is based on a rare coincidence of moral and strategic interests, the continuing tendency is to ignore Israel's growing potential as a permanent and multi-purpose access point indispensable to any Western security or defense structure. Dismissed is the possibility that in the event of an oil consumer-producer confrontation forced upon the West by extortionist oil prices, the presence in the Middle East of a strong Israel could prove to be of great value.

It is clear that the Soviet Union has long understood the vulnerability of the West because of its dependence on oil. The successful postwar effort by American multi-national oil corporations to expand their markets transformed Western Europe and Japan from a dependency on coal to oil and increased their future vulnerability to oil cutoffs. Soviet actions in the Middle East, beginning with massive arms shipments to Nasser in 1955 and subsequent penetration and overthrow of pro-Western regimes in Iraq, Yemen, Somalia and Libya, tend to strengthen Soviet power in a vital area. Soviet encouragement of the formation of OPEC, its call for ever higher oil prices, its championing of oil embargoes against the West, its acquisition of military, naval and airbase rights in the Mediterranean, Red and Arabian Seas, the Indian Ocean, the Persian Gulf and along the African coast threaten the economic, political and military security of the West. All such moves appear to indicate that the first major confrontation between the United States and the Soviet Union will be in the Middle East—over oil. Israel can act as a land route for supplies, as a refueling base, supply depot and tactical support arm for the United States in any such confrontation with the Soviet Union.

Although Israel acted in June 1967 for the protection of its own national interest, the fact remains that in the

1967–73 interwar period, Israel's military presence along the Suez in effect denied Soviet access to the Canal. Forgotten are the years when the Kremlin was forced to use the more cumbersome route around Africa to ship its supplies to North Vietnam—a considerable delay that resulted in diminished American losses.

Indeed, since June 1967 events have focused on Soviet-Egyptian attempts to return to the *status quo ante* and the twin American-Israeli objectives of deterrence and retention of the existing balance. It is against this perspective that one must view Nasser's War of Attrition, from March 1969 to August 1970 and the Yom Kippur War of October 1973 as developments in a continuing Arab and Soviet drama.

In both cases, the Israelis dramatically arrested the expansion of Soviet power. First in the sharpened contest for air superiority over the Suez Canal (July 1970), the line was drawn in a definitive manner, not by the United States but by Israel. The Israeli Air Force displayed not only a willingness to tangle with Soviet pilots, but a superior ability. This Israeli stand brought home to Moscow the threat of a collision with the United States—a factor in the subsequent Soviet "exodus" from Egypt in July 1972. It demonstrated the validity of the Nixon Doctrine that, backed by solid American support but without direct American intervention, a small state threatened by Soviet military action can deter the Soviets from precipitous action that would upset the regional balance.

Likewise, the Kremlin's role in the Yom Kippur War was primarily strategic: a bold and calculated attempt to render Arab states dependent on Soviet protection, to neutralize Europe, to undermine NATO and to drive the

United States out of the Mediterranean and the Middle East.[2]

While American support for Israel has been inaccurately described as facilitating Soviet penetration of the region, it has in fact helped preserve endangered pro-Western Arab regimes and lessened their need to depend militarily on the United States.

The clearest example of such aid was in September 1970, when Israeli action, requested by and closely co-ordinated with the United States, helped deter the Syrians, backed by the Soviets, from a full-scale invasion into Jordan.[3] Again, there is little doubt that were it not for repeated warnings by Israel, Syria would have intervened even more massively in the civil war between Christians and Muslims in Lebanon. Indeed, the restraint that Damascus demonstrates is surely conditioned by its sobering perception of Israeli strength and determination. It was only when the Christians failed to mobilize effective support on their side and the Arab world, with American acquiescence, sanctioned the Syrian takeover of Lebanon under the guise of a pan-Arab peacekeeping force, that Israel's deterrent influence was circumscribed.

At the regional level, it is important to stress that conflict and tension are endemic, a condition traceable largely to the sectarian and fragmented nature of Middle Eastern society. Territorial disputes among Arab states are persistent; ethnic and religious rivalries abound; conservative and radical attitudes concerning social change are continuously in conflict. All this illustrates that Arab countries, like so many Third World states, are inherently unstable—and therefore unreliable for oil resources and for our long-term diplomatic and strategic sustenance.

In the absence of an Arab-Israeli conflict, the Arab states themselves would sharply divide into two major hostile camps with a strong disposition to go for each other's jugular. The conservative monarchies would seek direct American protection against the Soviet-supported expansionist, militant states, including the terrorist movements. No longer shielded by an Israeli state bearing the brunt of any attack, the conservative regimes would require direct, large-scale military support—including American troops—to survive both overt and covert aggression promoted by Moscow. Ever since its establishment, Israel has served as a "lightning rod" for the oil-rich countries and the pro-Western regimes by diverting the attentions and energies of the Arab radicals away from them. For whatever reasons, American statesmen have been too timid to admit publicly that Israel, by virtue of its strategic location, was playing this positive role. Arab spokesmen, however, have made reference to it.

A corollary of this interest is the continuing need to maintain the balance of power in the Arab-Israeli zone. The conflict has emerged as a paramount test of American credibility and is closely monitored by all governments linked to the Western defense network. Upsetting the balance against Israel or allowing it to wobble would result in regional instability, erosion of credibility among allies, encouragement to adversaries to test further American credibility in other regions and divisive political turmoil at home. Clearly, abandonment of Israel would undermine the credibility of other commitments and, eventually, the underpinnings of the entire Western alliance structure. Unfortunately, this view is not shared by the majority of the "Arabists," the so-called experts on

34   *The Politics of Defeat*

the Middle East in the United States foreign policy establishment.

While certain "Arabists" might be understood to have a partisan or even prejudicial approach to our interests in the region, it is difficult to understand how they can carry on in ignorance of certain central facts. *What is important for them to keep in mind about the bond between Israel and America is that the volume of American military aid to Israel constitutes less than one percent of the United States defense budget and that Israel is a priceless strategic stronghold, a reliable anti-Communist bastion, an essential contingency base and a crucial link in the NATO defense posture.*

Only those more concerned with a narrow interpretation of Israel's needs rather than America's, or, alternately, those concerned about maintaining for Israel some virgin neutral position "untainted" by the power struggle between East and West could overlook such critical considerations. Israel is in fact so much of a national security bargain for America that we sometimes underestimate not only her reality, but even more importantly, her true potential—a potential she would realize if only we would learn to nurture her properly.

II

MOSCOW'S DESIGNS FOR THE REGION

THE Soviet Union's attraction to the Middle East is based on the region's political instability, its economic and social problems and its critical importance to the industrial democracies. Accordingly, it is an area of challenging opportunity for the establishment of new power relationships in the world. Moscow has moved rapidly into the region and in two decades has made impressive gains. In 1954, the Soviets first accorded the Arab states the highest priority in military and economic aid. In June 1967, the Soviet Navy entered the Mediterranean in strength and in 1968 took up a permanent station in the Arabian Sea. In 1970, the Soviet Air Force arrived in Egypt. By 1971, an American president (Nixon) unfortunately thought it necessary to acknowledge that the Soviets had acquired important "interests" in the region and that a lasting Arab-Israeli settlement would have to take those interests into account.

As an inviting vacuum, the Middle East has long been the object of European diplomacy. Indeed, the central and recurrent theme of European diplomacy through the nineteenth century had been the rivalry between the land power of Russia and the sea power of Great Britain for dominance in the Middle East, then under the control of the Ottoman Empire. Victorian and Edwardian Britain called this struggle the "Eastern Question." It became the major focus in the maintenance of the balance of power in Europe. Since the Middle East is less accessible by land from the north and more open to naval penetration, the Western European powers succeeded in establishing a firmer foothold in the region than did Tsarist Russia in its southward expansion into Turkey and Iran. World War I and the subsequent demise of the Ottoman Empire "resolved" this issue in favor of Britain and France. Russia, because of its internal convulsions resulting from the Bolshevik Revolution, had neither the capability nor the will to continue its imperial ambitions. Preoccupied with internal affairs and the reemergence of Germany, the Soviet leaders assuaged themselves throughout the interwar period with the defunct Leninist doctrine of the inevitable collapse of imperialist capitalism and made no significant attempts at inroads into the region now dominated by the British and French through a system of mandates and preferential alliances.

Soviet politico-military interests in the Middle East began to intensify even before the Second World War, with the German-Soviet Pact of August 1939. Soviet demands on Iran and Turkey during and immediately following the war highlighted these interests. Moscow's political offensive in both countries marked a return to the Tsarist policies of territorial expansion.

The conclusion of the Second World War sparked the resurgence of nationalist demands for unqualified independence. The momentum shifted to "disimperialism," yet the withdrawal from established positions was an uneven and protracted process, complicated by the exigencies of the East-West cold war. For here, too, geography remained a fundamental determinant in Western strategic thinking: the proximity of the Middle East region to the Soviet Union and the fear of Communist aggression; the central importance of the Suez Canal and the route to Asia; the denial of the north-south land route to the Soviet Union; the safeguarding of fabulous oil deposits for the West; and finally the protection of NATO's southern flank.

Nevertheless, the most pressing postwar requirement in the Middle East was for reconciliation between the various forms of indigenous nationalism and the Western powers. For Iran and Turkey, countries contiguous to the Soviet Union, the problem was precipitated by the return of traditionalist Tsarist policies of encroachment even before the conclusion of the war. Soviet postwar pressure took the form of a civil war in Greece, demands for bases in the Turkish Straits and for the annexation of parts of eastern Turkey and support of separatist movements in northwestern Iran. Both Greece and Turkey held firm and with Western help were able to induce Soviet withdrawal. The new series of Soviet moves led successively to the Truman Doctrine,[1] the extension of

NATO to Turkey, the creation of the Baghdad Pact and the positioning of the Sixth Fleet in the Mediterranean. The end result of the Soviet drive, therefore, was to bring American power into the region.

Had the Soviets succeeded in subordinating Turkey and Iran, they would have been able to thrust their naval and air power into the Mediterranean and Arabian seas through unimpeded routes. In that event, the Soviet Union might have challenged the supremacy of the West on both sides of the Suez Canal while eliminating any potential threat to Soviet security from southwest Asia. As it turned out, however, instead of having forward Russian bases, the Soviet Union faced on its southern flank a pro-Western military alignment.

By contrast, the Soviets have scored heavily in Arab countries for a number of reasons. No Arab state borders on the Soviet Union. Therefore Arabs, unlike Turks and Persians, had never experienced Russian overland military imperialism. Then too, in the interwar period, when the region was under the direct and indirect control of Britain and France, the Arab countries were deprived of the educational experiences which diplomatic and consular relations with the Soviets inevitably foster.

Up to the end of 1948, the Soviet postwar effort in the region focused inevitably on exploiting the opportunity for maximum gain and political influence in Iran and Turkey. It is difficult, however, to explain the relatively limited activity of the Soviet Union in the Arab areas in the 1948–1955 period.[2] The Soviets may have considered the region of low priority or ill-suited for an ideological offensive. Stalin considered the Arabs backward and feudal and ordered that no help be given to them. Perhaps the Soviets chose to rely on existing intra-regional tensions and on the anti-Western posture of Arab leaders to preclude the success of the ongoing Anglo-American efforts to "organize" the area.

Trading on Arab-Israeli friction and on Western efforts to draw Arabs into a regional security pact, the Soviets, through Czechoslovakia, concluded their first arms agreement with Egypt in 1955 and thus emerged as a major power in the region.[3] Interestingly, this move was made indirectly through Czechoslovakia because Moscow recognized that the region was a Western preserve. Though Moscow's probing action was in violation of a tacit understanding governing respective spheres of influence, it was met with no adequate Western response. This Western failure to protect its interests enabled the Soviets to "leapfrog" the Baghdad Pact, which became CENTO after the Iraqi revolution of July 1958, and to confront their southern neighbors from the rear. The arms pact not only marked the beginning of East-West rivalry for influence in the Arab East, but also shattered the power balance achieved by the Tripartite Declaration of 1950 in which the United States, Britain and France had pledged to ration the supply of arms to the Arab-Israeli zone so as to avoid an arms race.

Exploiting both Arab-Israeli friction and Western efforts to organize the Baghdad Pact, the Soviets gained in Egypt and moved toward involvement with other Arab states. They were aided, as we have seen, by Arab inexperience with Russia. While the Turks and Persians had the Russian military presence by land, the Arab experience with imperialism had been of the salt-water variety: the European maritime and commercial presence.

Consequently, fear of the Russian bear had to be learned the hard way.

It is a reductive fallacy that Soviet penetration is the consequence of the Arab-Israeli issue. This proposition ignores not only the radical nature of Arab nationalism, but also a number of developments that combined to give the Soviet Union its historic opportunity for greater influence in the region. It also discounts the British decision to withdraw "east of Suez," the actual French withdrawal from NATO and from naval bases in Tunisia and Algeria, the problem of Cyprus with its attendant Greek-Turkish tensions, the Arab-Iranian rivalry in the Gulf, the Yemeni, Iraqi and Sudanese civil conflicts and the highly successful Soviet policy of accommodation with Iran and Turkey. All these developments created new opportunities for the achievement of Russia's ambitions in the Middle East.

Soviet policy came to focus preeminently on relations with the Arab states, particularly after Albania's defection to the Chinese camp and after efforts to win back Yugoslavia had failed. The Soviets aided themselves immensely by sympathizing with and actively exploiting Arab hostility toward Israel. To some observers, the entire Soviet effort in the Arab countries since 1955 appeared to be directed mainly at gaining leverage over Iran and Turkey as part of the general thrust in the direction of the Persian Gulf and the Turkish Straits. From a broader perspective, however, Soviet activities could have been seen as directed, in their first phase, at the neutralization of the United States Sixth Fleet and the outflanking of NATO forces in the Mediterranean and Western Europe. Having accomplished that, they could turn their attention to China.

The absence of any critical examination of either the impact of technology upon geopolitics or the increasing dependence of the West on Middle Eastern oil seemed strange in the light of what was surely the most conspicuous change in the region's strategic environment: the escalation of Soviet naval power in the eastern Mediterranean and the end of the exclusive domination of those waters by a single power. The Soviet Union's emphasis on the projection of seapower beyond its customary bounds revealed the Soviet objective of attaining greater mobility for strategic and conventional forces. Closure of the Suez Canal had for a time complicated both the Soviet supply line to North Vietnam and the creation of a strategic relationship with India.

Nevertheless, the expansion of Soviet naval deployment always served a number of strategic purposes. It was necessary to provide a means for the surveillance of the NATO fleet, as well as a capability to attack NATO nuclear strike ships in the event of general war. It was also required in order to increase the credibility of the Soviet strategic deterrent to possible United States defensive actions against lower-level Soviet designs.

The acquisition of strategic mobility and a wide-ranging, self-sufficient naval force serves to expand Soviet diplomatic and military options in the Third World. To preempt the United States and China—its principal rivals —the Soviet Union must acquire even greater strategic mobility and also secure a strategic relationship with India. Achieving these ends, in turn, requires the extension of lines of communication through the Middle East, along the shores of the Red Sea and the Persian Gulf and into East Africa.

If firmly established along this littoral, with access to port and other facilities, the Soviets could threaten the routes of the West to Suez and beyond, bypass the Canal and seek to cut the link between NATO and its Asian allies.

Meanwhile, the Soviets were also seeking greater mobility for their conventional forces. It was, indeed, for the achievement of conventional political ends that the Soviets expanded their naval power and are now pursuing an aggressive Middle East policy. Moscow has wanted to pose a formidable threat to NATO and, counting precisely on Western tolerance, has intensified its efforts.

As Moscow projected its seapower beyond customary bounds, strategic thinkers in America asked only marginal questions and often reached unfounded conclusions. The larger and more important questions were ignored. Instead, apologists for Soviet behavior manufactured theories to justify or explain the escalating Soviet naval presence in both the Mediterranean and the Indian Ocean as reasonable expectations. Indeed, left to themselves, the apologists would have it both ways: United States naval power is provocative, but escalating Soviet seapower is reactive; the Mediterranean is no longer vital for mounting or countering a threat to the Soviet homeland, but the purpose of Soviet naval power is to defend against Western strategic attack. On the one hand, the development of nuclear technology removes the necessity for forward positions, but on the other, Moscow's naval deployment into the Indian Ocean is seen only as a reaction to our presumed submarine-based nuclear threat against Russian missile and space industries in Central Asia. Left unexplained is the unremitting Soviet drive for strategic bases in Egypt, Syria, South Yemen, Mozambique, Somalia and Angola, and the continued Soviet naval presence in the Indian Ocean—of paramount importance to the West.

Also ignored among the reasons for the Soviet presence in the Indian Ocean are Moscow's interest in excluding Chinese influence from that region and its desire to cultivate positions of strength along the waterway used for the transportation of Persian Gulf oil to the industrial democracies. For the apologists, the fact that the Soviet naval presence in the Indian Ocean began very soon after the announcement of the British intention to withdraw east of Suez is merely a historical coincidence.

Ignored too is the fact that while the Soviet Union gives as its rationale for its growing naval presence in the Indian Ocean the need to counter the presumed American sea-borne missile threat, there is almost no Soviet anti-submarine warfare capability in that region. The fact that the number of Soviet ship days in the Indian Ocean exceeds that of the United States by more than three to one is also overlooked. In point of fact the Soviet emphasis is on oceanographic research, aimed at making Soviet submarine activities less detectable by charting the blind zones in which sonar techniques of submarine location are rendered inaccurate and ineffective.

From the Soviet vantage, the Middle East is more accurately the Near South. Its access to the Red Sea is direct from the Black Sea, through the Turkish Straits and Suez. With the Suez Canal blocked, however, access must be gained through more cumbersome routes—through Gibraltar and around Africa, or easterly, around Asia and its subcontinent. Just one glance at a world map will show that the Red Sea with the Canal closed is about the farthest point in the world from the Soviet Union by sea. The reopened Canal has allowed the Soviets to shorten their lines of communication from the Black Sea to the Red Sea, the Persian Gulf and the Indian Ocean. The distance between Odessa and Aden via the Suez Canal is 2,500 miles, as opposed to 11,500 miles via the Cape. Vladivostok to Aden is 7,700 miles. This added naval flexibility affords Moscow an additional capacity to influence policies of littoral states. If at any stage the Soviets believed that they could act quickly and decisively in a changing situation without provoking Western reaction, they would be able to do so.

Their growing familiarity with port areas in the region could be of considerable assistance to them in such a situation. Intimate knowledge of the physical plans of bases, airfields and ports either because they had built them or because they had operated them at some point or another would become a significant consideration in determining the military option in a moment of need. Development of military infrastructures for subsequent intervention is a favorite Soviet method of penetration too often overlooked by so-called experts. Irrespective of whether or not the Soviets operate bases or merely have access to such facilities, they are in a position to intervene militarily in a crisis situation with or without the consent of the countries concerned.*

The fact that the region is the Soviet Union's "Near South" brings a significant strategic weight to bear on

---

* A good example of how important this kind of information can be is the Entebbe raid. Had the Israelis not constructed the Entebbe airport in Uganda themselves, they might not have had the knowledge of facilities necessary to execute their daring operation in rescuing the PLO-held hostages there in July 1976.

the world geopolitical scene. In the 1970 Jordanian crisis, the Soviets were able to treble the missile capability of their fleet in just thirty hours while it took ten days to assemble the Kennedy aircraft carrier group.

Soviet land-based air power in Egypt, easily repro- visioned from the Russian heartland, was intended among other things to nullify the protective air shield of the Sixth Fleet. Without air superiority based on the two carriers of the fleet, the entire United States force is vulnerable. Having originally challenged Western sea- borne power in the Mediterranean from these land bases in Egypt, the Soviet Union is today capable of using its naval power alone to impose constraints on the operations of the Sixth Fleet.

Despite Russia's close proximity to the Middle East, and centuries of Byzantine scheming for control of the region, Moscow has on a number of occasions miscalcu- lated the dynamics of the region. Unfortunately, the United States has not known how to gain full advantage from these Soviet failures.

The most notable Soviet miscalculation was in fabri- cating reports alleging Israeli mobilization against Syria in May 1967, thereby triggering a series of Egyptian responses which led to the Six Day War. Israel's dramatic victories in June 1967 not only reversed her prewar stra- tegic position vis-à-vis Egypt, Syria and Jordan, but also severely damaged Soviet prestige. Her new borders on the banks of the Suez, the Jordan River and the Golan Heights provided security in depth and an ideal defense against conventional aggression. Yet—despite the new regional equation—negotiations for peace did not follow, precisely because of Soviet arms replenishment. Immediately following the Arab defeat, large-scale Soviet arms shipments—by air and by sea—poured into Egypt and Syria and, to a lesser degree, Iraq. There was every indication that Moscow would restore the arms inventories of its client states to prewar levels in all categories. Nevertheless, some American observers still viewed Soviet objectives as moot and even beneficial. While some understood that Soviet replenishment was designed primarily to forestall an Arab-Israeli *modus vivendi* that might otherwise have evolved, others couched their forecasts only in conjectural terms, not in keeping with the stark realities of the situation. Appraisals were put forward as though the series of major arms deals were in no way related to Moscow's systematic exploitation of the Arab-Israeli conflict for the purpose of supplanting Western influence in the entire area.

Even more worrisome was the presumption of the much heralded Soviet "dilemma," which purportedly resulted from a concern to avoid another Arab-Israeli war because of its possible escalation into a confrontation with the United States. Dismissed was the dissenting view that massive Soviet training and supplies were meant to sustain Middle East tension and narrow the chances for Arab realism and recognition of Israel. Moreover, hostilities, even those leading to Israeli victories, would deepen the dependence of the Arab states on Soviet protection.

Assumptions of Soviet restraint in the supply of advanced weapons were proved to be in error. The resupply effort accelerated steadily until Egyptian and then Syrian combat losses in equipment were largely replaced. Then Soviet emphasis shifted to more advanced aircraft, air defense and intensive Soviet training in every aspect of military planning and operations. Egypt's intensive artillery bombardment of Israeli canal positions beginning in the autumn of 1968 was the inevitable result of massive Soviet logistic support and marked the first phase of Egypt's effort to create new tension and generate Western pressure on Israel. This led to Nasser's formal rejection of the cease-fire and to the war of attrition, April 1969 to August 1970.

It was another serious error to assume—as some did—that Moscow would not seek base agreements and would avoid defense pacts in the Middle East. The Soviets finessed this issue by gradually establishing *de facto* bases for air and naval units which both supported the Arabs and facilitated their own activities to counter the presence of the United States Sixth Fleet.

A third error was the assumption that the Soviets encouraged Egyptian moderation. This was quickly negated by the "no peace, no recognition, no negotiations" formula adopted at the Khartoum Conference in August 1967, marking the beginning of a Soviet-Egyptian diplomatic offensive to sustain high tension in the Arab-Israeli zone. As events were to show, the only "moderation" the Soviets encouraged was periodically to try to restrain Arab offensive activity—since the Arabs had not yet reached the level of training and capability for successful military operations.

Modern Soviet policy takes a longer view than most Western analysts would like to recognize. Moscow exploited such narrow vision with intensified efforts in the Middle East, which it regarded as the major arena in which to forge new power relationships in the world. It is indeed only in this area that Moscow has shown a willingness to commit military force in support of political goals.

Immediately after the Arab defeat of 1967, the Soviet Union rearmed Egypt to thwart any possible movement toward a *modus vivendi* between Arabs and Israel. In return, Egypt gave the Soviet Mediterranean fleet storage and repair facilities—the equivalent of naval base rights— at Alexandria and Port Said and allowed Soviet pilots to fly their planes with Egyptian markings on missions over the Mediterranean—the equivalent of rights to Egyptian air bases.[4] With the flow of Soviet weapons a constant source of encouragement, Egypt showed little inclination toward political settlement.

In the autumn of 1968, the Egyptians began an intensive artillery bombardment of Israeli positions on the east bank of the Suez Canal. To the Israelis, the Egyptians appeared more interested in forcing a partial withdrawal with their newly acquired strength in artillery than in bolstering their diplomatic bargaining posture. Until then, only a small number of Israeli troops held the canal, reflecting hopes for a diplomatic breakthrough. To gain urgently needed respite for strengthening its defenses, Israel then embarked on a series of helicopter-borne commando raids against bridges, dams and power lines deep inside Egyptian territory. The relative ease with which the Israeli Air Force penetrated Egyptian air space temporarily stunned Cairo and forced the Egyptians to cease the shelling and disperse their forces. The Israelis were thus able to construct the Bar-Lev Line—a network of fortifications, facilities and underground bunkers reinforced by rail from the Cairo-Gaza railway line. By the time Egypt finally overcame its fear of the commando raids and resumed its bombardments along the canal, the Bar-Lev Line had been completed.[5]

By then, also, the Egyptian army had concluded an unprecedented reorganization and a program of training under the supervision of Soviet experts. A new spirit of confidence now pervaded the officer corps, and Abdel Nasser found himself caught in a dilemma between the impatient demands of his officers to cross the canal and the cautious counsel of his Soviet advisors, who still believed that Israel could be compelled by political pressure to withdraw from the canal. His Chief of Staff, General Abdel Muneim Riad, convinced Nasser that operations in restricted areas best suited to Egypt might succeed. As a possible preliminary for a canal crossover sometime during the summer of 1969, this new offensive began on 8 March 1969 with some 10,000 artillery shells landing on the Israeli lines and more than 35,000 in the days immediately following.

On 1 April, Nasser disavowed the cease-fire agreement of 1967 and formally launched his war of attrition. Its purpose was to take advantage of Egypt's numerical superiority in manpower and artillery along the canal and inflict heavy casualties on Israel. This would not only force Israel to mobilize more of her reserves but also undermine her economic capacity to sustain war.[6] The effect of massive shellings and commando forays across the canal was to send the Israeli casualty rate spiralling upward. By the summer of 1969, the Israeli casualty rate stood at 70 per month along the canal alone, in addition to casualties from bombardment in the Jordan Valley and the actions of guerrilla-terrorists. From the standpoint of its size and population, Israel regarded an indefinite

continuation of this casualty rate prohibitive. Furthermore, the shelling made it more difficult to supply the
fortifications, much less repair the damage caused by
the shelling.

Meanwhile, there were growing indications that Nasser,
as in 1967, was again beginning to get carried away with
local success. The immediate problem was casualties, but
the Israelis did not rule out an Egyptian crossing of the
canal, even though control of the air seemed to preclude
that eventuality. Confronted with the necessity of solving
a pressing tactical problem, Israel decided to employ
air power as the most effective and economic means of
balancing the war of attrition and deterring a wider war
that might trigger a possible collision of the superpowers.
Air power served both as a long-range tactical weapon
and as a short-term solution for day-to-day problems. But
to neutralize the Egyptian artillery, the Israeli Air Force
had first to eliminate the antiaircraft positions, including
the SAM sites that defended gun lines and troop positions
along the canal. Accordingly, on 20 July 1969, Israel
sent its air force into action on a regular basis, as it had
against Arab artillery and guerrilla strongholds in Jordan
and in Syria.[7]

Not since the Six Day War had Israeli jets been dispatched on ground attack missions in the canal sector.
Until then, air combat had been held to a relative minimum. In the period between the end of the Six Day
War and 20 July 1969, Israel had claimed kills of 26
Egyptian MIG-19 and MIG-21 fighters. The July action
marked the escalation of hostilities and the turning point
in the war of attrition. Five times during the week of
20 to 27 July, Israeli planes in Sinai streaked across the

canal to make bombing and strafing runs from Port Said in the north to Port Suez in the south, and three times the Egyptian Air Force reacted. On each occasion the Egyptians ignored Israeli planes and headed straight for installations behind Israeli lines. Air battles ensued, however, and by the end of the week the score, according to Israeli accounts, was 12 Egyptians and 2 Israeli jets downed, some by ground fire on both sides. Israel also reported that it had destroyed or damaged six missile sites, a radar station, and scores of gun emplacements.

Thus, the first attempt of the rebuilt Egyptian Air Force to challenge Israeli air superiority since the Six Day War failed. In the space of one week, the Israeli Air Force proved that Egypt clearly lacked the air power necessary to support a major ground offensive across the Suez Canal into Sinai. Thereafter, Egypt concentrated on intensified local attacks on Israeli positions along the canal and on shallow penetration of Israeli air space with low-level, hit-and-run air strikes.

In committing the Israeli Air Force to daily action on the Egyptian front and by refining its role in the postwar fighting, Israel took the initiative in the war of attrition. It now placed greater emphasis on air power to balance Cairo's tactics and, possibly, to restore the cease-fire along the Suez Canal. After a series of major air battles, Israel's air superiority permitted a spectacular amphibious operation along the Egyptian coast of the Gulf of Suez in September. Exploiting the element of surprise, an Israeli armored force, accompanied by infantry and strong air support, landed on the Egyptian coast from assault craft and, in a ten-hour operation, cut a swath some 50 kilometers in length along the coast. In the process, it destroyed radar and antiaircraft installations protecting the approaches to Egypt from the Gulf of Suez. The complete absence of Egyptian land, sea or air forces, other than those directly engaged by the Israelis, proved that the Egyptian line could be outflanked and that Cairo itself was not safe from an armored thrust.

Israeli leaders believed that by maintaining access to the Egyptian interior, they could neutralize from the air any massive buildup behind Egyptian lines. Thus, in highlighting the increased Israeli Air Force involvement in the Suez Canal and Sinai sectors on the eve of the amphibious thrust, General Bar-Lev declared that Israeli air strikes had postponed a new war with Egypt and served to decrease Egyptian military activity along the Suez Canal.[8] The ratio of Israeli to Egyptian losses was impressive. In the period between 20 July and 8 September 1969, the Israeli Air Force carried out nearly 1,000 sorties into Egyptian territory at a cost of three aircraft, as compared with 100 Egyptian sorties into Israeli territory at a cost of 21 aircraft. On the other hand, the Israeli chief of staff conceded that Israel was unable to force the Egyptians to maintain an absolute cease-fire.

Nevertheless, the Israeli Air Force continued to employ Skyhawk bombers to pound Egyptian artillery and widen the gap created by the destruction of antiaircraft defenses. On 10 November, a high-ranking Israeli official declared that all Egyptian ground-to-air missile sites along the Suez Canal had been destroyed in two months of air strikes. The statement confirmed that the entire 250-mile Egyptian front, from Port Said on the Mediterranean coast to the Red Sea, lacked ground-to-air missile defense against attack. Israeli strategy seemed to imply that the whole of

Egypt was fair game to the Israeli Air Force. In terms
of relieving the pressure on the Bar-Lev line, the summer
and autumn air offensives against Egyptian artillery and
against radar and missile sites along the Suez front had
been highly successful. Israeli casualties dropped dramatically from 106 in July to 30 during the month of
December.[9] Moreover, in December 1969, Gamal Abdel
Nasser admitted at the Arab summit conference in Rabat
that Egypt lacked the capability of waging all-out war.

On 7 January 1970, Israel embarked on its new strategy
of deep penetration bombing at the heart of Egypt. The
arrival of the first F-4 Phantom jets during September
1969 considerably enhanced her capability to carry out
these operations. The Israeli Air Force had now entered
a new period of absolute proved superiority, plane for
plane and pilot for pilot, that had not existed in the past.
Moreover, the Phantom aircraft were highly suited to
Israel's concept of offensive strategy—itself the outgrowth
of Israel's psychological disposition. Specifically, the Phantom's excellence as a fighter-bomber was best suited for
extending attacks of political and military significance into
the strategically vulnerable Nile Delta.

The new strategy had several alternative objectives.
Militarily, it aimed at easing Egyptian pressure along
the canal and at further deterring the Egyptians from
contemplating a cross-canal invasion. Politically, the Israelis gave Nasser the choice of tolerating continued
deep-penetration raids, with all the implications of such
a choice for his regime, or reinstating the cease-fire, either
tacitly or openly. Other political and strategic objectives,
though never officially defined, probably included breaking Egyptian morale, creating a credibility gap between

Nasser and the Egyptian people, precipitating the down-fall of the Nasser regime or forcing a major change in Egyptian foreign policy.[10]

However, the outcome of Israel's experiment in the use of air power to achieve political and diplomatic objectives was different from what had been expected. The evidence suggests that the Israeli bombing of Egypt proper had enhanced rather than impaired Egyptian morale. Many sources nevertheless believed that Nasser's regime faced imminent collapse. After some time the Israelis at least began to doubt this possibility; moreover, Nasser himself probably realized that the bombing was not menacing his political position in Egypt. The Egyptian leader chose neither to restore the cease-fire nor to negotiate. In a secret visit to Moscow, he requested an even more direct and active Soviet role in the air defense of Egypt.

Moscow's decision to assume such a responsibility, even in piecemeal fashion, and its willingness to face the uncertainties of military interposition, necessarily raised the risk of confrontation with the United States. Yet this development was but a logical continuation in the erosion of the ground rules of limited war—a process initiated by the local protagonists in the unremitting conduct of their rival strategies of attrition and deep-penetration bombing.

On 18 March 1970, United States sources confirmed that the Soviet Union had begun the delivery to Egypt of large numbers of SAM-3s capable of dealing with low-flying aircraft. Introduction of the SAM-3s and their initial deployment in the Egyptian interior marked the first phase in a progression of escalating military steps undertaken directly by the Soviet Union. The second phase came in mid-April when Russian pilots in MIG-21Js began active combat patrols over the heartland of Egypt. This, in turn, released Egyptian pilots for offensive missions over the Suez and Sinai areas.

Through these Soviet moves, the Suez war reached a new and unpredictable phase. The Soviet Union had stationed an entire air defense brigade in Egypt comprised of Soviet-manned SAM-3 antiaircraft missile batteries and between 100 and 200 Soviet pilots—who provided their own air umbrella for the SAM-3s. The Israeli response was to delineate the front-line area in the war of attrition by agreeing not to attack Alexandria, Port Said or Aswan. Attacks in the Cairo area had ceased earlier, on 17 February 1970. Israel indicated that its air force would avoid direct confrontation with Soviet pilots so long as they stayed clear of the vital 25-mile strip west of the canal. The Israeli Air Force would continue its operation in this area as part of Israel's immediate defense zone. Thus, the first result of the Soviet introduction of the SAM-3s, as well as Soviet pilots, was a more precise definition of the area in which the Israeli Air Force would operate to offset Egypt's superiority in artillery and ground forces. The Soviet military presence released additional Egyptian resources for the war of attrition and made it unnecessary for Egypt to disperse its forces. The overall effect was to increase the concentration of resources and firepower in the combat zone. This, in turn, forced Israel to search for countermeasures in the war of attrition.

Soviet reluctance to challenge the Israeli Air Force in the so-called free zone along the Suez Canal tacitly affirmed the Soviet Union's acceptance of the Israeli proposal. The first test came after a highly successful Egyptian commando raid in the vulnerable northern section of the canal. In retaliation, the Israeli Air Force unleashed heavy attacks on Egyptian positions north of Kantara on 30 May 1970. Soviet pilots did not venture into the Suez combat zone, and the Israelis thereafter unleashed daily bombardments of 10 to 15 hours duration along the entire Suez Canal region.

Despite the increased Soviet military presence, the Israelis regained the initiative, if only in the immediate combat zone. With Soviet efforts to extend the ground-to-air missile network from the Egyptian interior to the battle zone, however, the pendulum began to swing in the opposite direction. As early as 19 May 1970, reliable sources reported that the Soviets were building 15 T-shaped SAM-3 concrete shelter sites, spaced at 7½-mile intervals along the entire 100-mile length of the Suez Canal.[11] On 30 June, Israeli reconnaissance detected a new, interlocking 17-mile-deep Egyptian air defense belt. This area included improved high-altitude SAM-2s and low-altitude SAM-3s, supported by more than 1,000 conventional antiaircraft weapons and Soviet technicians. This new deployment in the central sector straddled the imaginary red line running 25 miles west of the canal and brought the missile concentration, including the SAM-3s, into the Suez combat zone. The Suez war had reached an even more ominous stage.[12] The Soviets now entered the battle as a direct belligerent and escalated the conflict to a new level.

With the establishment of the new Egyptian air defense system along the southern and central sectors of the canal, a reevaluation of the SAM-2 missiles became necessary.

The Soviets concentrated the missiles in "packs" of mutually overlapping supporting positions. Another concentration of conventional antiaircraft batteries protected the missile system. These batteries consisted primarily of rapid-fire triple gun mounts, many of them directed by radar. Since they were concentrated in packs, the improved SAM-2 missiles could be launched in volleys, as compared with their previous single firings. They could also be fired from temporary sites in contrast to the earlier well-constructed and easily detected concrete emplacements.

Extension of the ground-to-air missile network from the Egyptian heartland to the canal area was inevitable because the Soviet buildup continued from March through June without vigorous censure from the United States. From the beginning, Israeli strategists, unlike their American counterparts, strongly contested the view that the Soviet Union had installed the SAM-3s and introduced air squadrons for defensive purposes.[13] Indeed, by regarding the missiles as "defensive," the American analysts accorded a degree of license to the Soviet military presence, and Moscow interpreted it in this light. However, the Israelis saw clearly that the Soviet Union had moved neither by mistake nor force of circumstance into direct military involvement in the Arab-Israeli conflict. On the contrary, Soviet involvement over the years, and especially in the preceding months, was deliberate, provocative and boldly calculated to confront Israel, the United States and other Western interests with high risk.

The absence of a positive American response to Israel's request for additional aircraft was interpreted by Moscow as a sign that it might intensify hostilities without hindrance. Regrettably, this interpretation was correct. The new missile deployment marked the third phase of direct Soviet involvement in support of Egypt's offensive attrition strategy.[14] It was an attempt to upset the status quo, not to stabilize it. At the least, neutralization of Israel's air superiority in the combat zone would presage intensification of the war of attrition; at the most, it would be the opening phase of an offensive to push back the lines and reopen the Suez Canal unilaterally. Inasmuch as any crossing of the Canal presupposed at least neutralization of the Israeli Air Force, Egyptian plans depended entirely on parallel Russian moves.

The emerging pattern was a gradual edging forward of the antiaircraft missile system to a point sufficient to cover the air space above the Israeli forward line with missile fire and, at the same time, keep the missile sites beyond the effective range of Israeli artillery. The Soviets had the capability to probe even further without the appearance of escalation. They could position the SAM-3s outside the 25-mile free zone and still threaten Israeli planes operating within the zone. To a far greater extent than in previous Soviet initiatives, the challenge to Israeli control of the air threatened to bring a dramatic shift in the regional power balance, which since 1967 had prevented the outbreak of full-scale hostilities.

At this juncture, Israel confronted a choice between heavy losses in continued air operations to hold the front line and the risk of crossing the imaginary red line to hit Soviet missiles. It was not a question of whether the established strategy of forward defense and retaliation enhanced or impaired Israeli security.

The problem grew more complex when Israeli leaders

realized that the new missile challenge required additional strike aircraft and advanced electronic equipment, neither of which appeared forthcoming. On the mistaken assumption that Moscow was ready to bargain diplomatically with regard to the regional power balance, the urgent American objective became not the elimination of the missile zone but a political solution that supposedly would satisfy both local protagonists. Therefore, when Israel requested an additional 100 to 150 Phantoms and 100 Skyhawks, the United States government held the purchase "in abeyance" and sought renewed negotiations between Israel and Egypt. Although all concerned parties, including the Soviet Union, had rejected American Secretary of State William Rogers's plan in December 1969, it now reappeared in capsule form as a "new initiative" linked to a proposed 90-day standstill cease-fire agreement.

The Israeli premier had earlier categorically rejected a limited cease-fire agreement, believing that termination of the air strikes would allow time for the badly bruised Egyptian army to regroup and for the Russians to establish their missile line. Israel had considered a limited cease-fire arrangement a threat to her freedom of action in the air over the combat zone. But once the Russians abandoned their policy of first building hardened sites for the missiles and switched to the tactic of deploying clusters of mobile missile launchers, the Israelis in the absence of needed equipment could do little to prevent their advance. Even as the Israeli Air Force continued to bomb the heavy concentrations of Egyptian artillery in other sectors of the canal to ease the pressure on the front line, it recognized that its air superiority was in jeopardy. Neither the Phantom nor the Skyhawk could survive the new missile deployment without incurring heavy losses, for which replacement had now become problematical.[15]

Two Israeli jets were lost on 30 June 1970. One was lost on 7 July, another on 18 July and a fifth aircraft was downed only two days before the cease-fire became effective on 7 August. On the other hand, the Israeli jets shot down five Russian-piloted MIG-21s on 30 July in the last major air battle above the Suez before the cease-fire. Israel did not publicize the air clash at the time in order to prevent increased tensions. Also, on 6 August, the last day before the cease-fire, Israel revealed that the Israeli Air Force had dropped more bombs than it had on any day since the Six Day War. For 79 days, the Israelis had conducted a total of 3,500 bombing sorties and inflicted losses on the Egyptian forces estimated at 10,000 dead and wounded, as well as substantial losses in equipment. Events indicated that the Soviets had reached the upper limits threatening great-power confrontation. Yet if the air war had receded to the same border perimeter that contained the ground forces it was largely due to American unwillingness to underwrite Israeli aircraft losses.

The United States political initiative, dating from June 1970, now seemed the only option available to Israel. It asked two things of Israel: to once again test the intentions of Moscow and Cairo in indirect talks and to risk a limited cease-fire despite the prospect of its being exploited. Jerusalem's initial hesitation was prompted principally by the risk it was required to take with respect to the cease-fire. After all, the Security Council resolution of 1967 had called for an unlimited and unconditional cease-fire. Nor could Israel overlook the indirect talks which had failed before, refusal of the Arabs to meet face to face with Israel as part of their non-recognition policy and the Soviet-Egyptian reference to a "political solution," not a genuine peace settlement.

Nevertheless, because of the intense pressures, the most telling of which was the tacit American threat to cut off the supply of Phantom jets, Israel agreed in August 1970 to accept the American initiative.[16] Against its inclination, the Israeli government agreed to a series of unilateral concessions in an effort to get the talks started. Israel accepted the procedure of indirect negotiation, agreed to a limited cease-fire, agreed to New York as the site of the talks and agreed not to make an issue out of the Arab refusal to delegate their foreign ministers to the talks as United Nations mediator Gunnar Jarring had requested.

Israel entered the cease-fire, only to find the Soviets and Egyptians immediately taking advantage of it to improve their missile defenses.[17] A cardinal provision of the agreement read: "Both sides will refrain from changing the military status quo within zones extending 50 kilometers (30 miles) to the east and the west of the cease-fire line. Neither side will introduce or construct any new military installations in these zones. Activities within the zone will be limited to the maintenance of existing installations at their present sites and positions and to the rotation and supply of forces presently within the zones." Israel's endorsement of the cease-fire was unconditional, and Moscow had given Washington a "categorical commitment" to abide by the restrictions.

On the night that the cease-fire went into effect, the agreement was violated by the Egyptians and the Soviets, who advanced their missile bases toward the Suez Canal. The United States had initiated the cease-fire, and Israel had agreed to it only after Washington had informed her that the Russians would abide by it.

These and further violations were announced by Israel, but not confirmed by the United States. On 16 August Secretary of Defense Melvin Laird stated that it was "very difficult to prove or disprove" the charges and that the United States government had no proof that promises had been broken. Two days later, the Soviets dismissed the Israeli allegations as "fabrications" and in the process quoted Secretary Laird. On 19 August Washington finally acknowledged a "forward deployment" but repeated that evidence of a continuing buildup was "not conclusive." It was not until 1 September that the United States government confirmed the violations. Confronted with a shift in the military balance, Israel had no alternative but to suspend her participation in the Jarring talks and demand the restoration of the military situation as it existed on 7 August, when the cease-fire agreement had gone into effect.

The dense missile system which Egypt, with Soviet connivance, had deployed in the standstill zone under the cease-fire screen altered the military balance and produced a threat that did not exist prior to 7 August. Moscow's power position in the Middle East was enhanced. *As for the United States, it failed to sustain its assurances that Israel would not suffer military disadvantage by the cease-fire. Washington thereby endangered the credibility of future American assurances.* The situation was redeemed only partly by agreeing to provide the arms shipments Washington had hoped to avoid in the first place.

Nevertheless, it must be noted that the manner in which the Soviets introduced missiles into the prohibited zone was designed to demonstrate that Moscow could violate agreements in the proved expectation that Washington would turn a blind eye to this breach of faith. After all, the Soviet move had been encouraged by the absence of an adequate American response to Nasser's denunciation of the 1967 cease-fire agreement and to the entire pattern of Soviet deployments from March to July 1970. Despite the American connection, Israel was forced to fight a largely Soviet-operated and integrated air defense system. What could not be won in war was achieved by duplicity. Egypt and the Soviet Union in fact exploited the American initiative by altering the military balance along the canal. Any subsequent Israeli withdrawal would have been viewed by the Arabs as Moscow's triumph in the Middle East. Moreover, the Soviets had proved that they could turn war on and off at will and without penalty. In fact, the cease-fire saved Egypt from having to acknowledge an unmitigated military defeat. Other important conclusions were drawn from the American reaction.

Egypt did not fail to conclude that while Moscow was prepared to sponsor wars, it could not deliver military victories without risking an open confrontation with the United States. Even the prevention of outright defeat was secured only at a heavy price—including that of mortgaging Egypt's sovereignty. The Soviet Union concluded that, surprisingly enough, the United States stood ready to prevent a total Egyptian collapse, if necessary even by restraining its one militarily proved client in the region, Israel. This was a profound lesson to be well applied by the Soviets and the Egyptians in their political planning for the Yom Kippur aggression only a short three years later.

Even as Moscow was consciously and actively preparing the stage for a new confrontation in the Arab-Israeli zone, it was also giving unprecedented emphasis to relations with the eastern part of the region, specifically, the approaches to eastern and southern Arabia, the Persian Gulf and the Indian Ocean—the outer lines of confrontation with China. As the subcontinent became the main arena of Russo-Chinese rivalry, the Red Sea and the Persian Gulf acquired new importance in Soviet strategy. Hence, prominent attention was given to ties with Syria, Iraq, Somalia and the two Yemens. Nevertheless, as the expanding Soviet presence was altering the region's strategic environment, certain analysts sought to minimize the nature of the challenge by overstating the dilemmas and limitations of a Soviet forward policy.

Events leading up to the Yom Kippur War are best viewed in the broad perspective of global politics. Egypt's acceptance of the August 1970 cease-fire, the Jordanian crackdown on the Palestinians and the death of Nasser in September were overshadowed by still greater events in 1972. These included the Sino-American rapprochement, intensification of the fighting in Vietnam, the Nixon-Brezhnev summit meeting in May and the "exodus" from Egypt of Soviet military advisors and combat personnel in July. It was generally believed that with fighting for the canal terminated, the Soviet military presence had become an intolerable burden for the Egyptians. Eventually this led to the departure of Soviet personnel. To be sure, the move was received with unreserved acclamation in the Egyptian army and satisfaction in Israel.

Few observers or analysts were able to discern any deeper or more crafty motives behind Anwar Sadat's move for the departure of Soviet forces in the second year of his presidency. While the Soviet departure seemed to provide temporary stability, it in fact created a situation more conducive to the outbreak of war, for it lessened Soviet motivation to curb the Egyptians. It is not mere coincidence that after the departure of Soviet forces from Egypt, joint communiques began to affirm the Arab right to use all possible means to recover their lands. Soviet readiness to support a military initiative should have been seen in inverse proportion to the risk that such action assumed. Only after a restructuring of the Soviet-Egyptian relationship into a form in which there was less danger of direct Soviet military entanglement could Sadat persuade Moscow to agree to the timing of the October 1973 attack. The Soviet restraint stemmed only from the concern to avoid direct involvement and did not apply to its furnishing military aid, guidance or advice to the Syrian and Egyptian armies. Indeed, President Sadat fully understood that Moscow objected only to direct Soviet participation in a cross-canal operation since that would have raised the threat of an American-Soviet confrontation.

At a time when most observers were inclined to exaggerate the strengthening of Soviet relations with Syria and Iraq as moves designed to counteract the impact of their supposedly declining influence in Egypt, Soviet-Egyptian collaboration actually accelerated in the wake of American failure to hold the diplomatic initiative for a Suez interim agreement. Lack of progress on this score contributed to Sadat's decision to prepare for war by turning to Moscow for military supplies. Pursuant to Syrian mediation on 28 September 1972, the Egyptian prime minister visited Moscow, and the joint communique issued on 17 October stated that "the Soviet side confirms once again that the Arab states are fully entitled to liberate their territory by diverse means." Soon thereafter, Soviet military advisors returned to Egypt. Obliged to renegotiate the instrument allowing Soviet access to certain facilities in Egyptian ports, the new Egyptian minister of war, Ahmed Ismail, visited Moscow in January 1973.

While the Soviets were preparing for war, the United States was holding discussions with Egypt, Jordan and Israel in the hope of preparing some of the groundwork for diplomatic movement after the Israeli elections scheduled for October. The lack of immediate results through the diplomatic route confirmed Sadat in his decision for war.[18] It is often said that for purposes of waging war Egypt turns to Russia, while in order to achieve "peace" she turns to America. What is not recognized is that America is also relied upon to deliver political gains from military defeat. In fact, this is the critical element in all Arab strategic planning for war.

During the six months leading up to October 1973, Soviet supplies accelerated in every category at an astonishing rate, leveling just before the Syrian-Egyptian attack and resuming shortly thereafter. In many instances, supplies represented the very type of hardware which supported the Syrian-Egyptian strategy. Moscow provided the improved model of the T-62 tank equipped with night-vision instrumentation, new armored personnel carriers, the all-weather and night-flying version of the MIG-21 (MF), the AT-3 SAGGER antitank missile system, the SA-6 mobile triple launchers, the SA-7 STRELA man-portable antiaircraft missile and the ZSU-23/4 anti-aircraft gun.

The major turning point in giving the Egyptians a new confidence in their own military capability was in March and April, when they began to receive the medium-range surface-to-surface SCUD B launchers whose missiles were capable of reaching Israeli population centers. Inasmuch as the SCUD provided the substitute for a medium-range bomber force and was thought necessary to deter possible Israeli deep penetration raids, Egypt's main requirement for going to war was satisfied.[19] Thus the final decision for war was made by the Soviets when they decided to supply the SCUD just three months before the second Nixon-Brezhnev 1973 summit conference.

Syria, too, began receiving the FROG surface-to-surface missile capable of reaching Israeli civilian targets. Furthermore, during the months of July and August 1973, Moscow rushed to Syria a surface-to-air missile system which in the Soviet view would neutralize Israeli air superiority along the front line. The intention was to neutralize the Israeli Air Force as the Arab forces advanced, while the SCUDs and FROGs would be poised against civilian targets as a deterrent to Israeli Air Force deep-penetration bombing attacks.

Continuing shipment of Soviet supplies and arrangements for political support, coupled with Egyptian coordination with Saudi Arabia for employment of the oil weapon, set the stage for war. Indeed, from mid-1972

onward, Egypt had been forging new links with Arab
states only subsequently revealed as a military coalition.
The innermost circle was comprised of Egypt, Syria and
Saudi Arabia; the intermediate circle included Kuwait,
Iraq, Sudan and Algeria; and the remainder formed the
outer circle. In point of fact, according to Sadat, an Egyptian attack had been planned for May 1973 but was
postponed because of the projected second Brezhnev-
Nixon summit conference.

When assessing the war scare of May 1973, observers
have given excessive weight to the "Basic Principles of
Relations Between The United States of America and The
Soviet Socialist Republic." This document, embracing the
principles of detente, was signed by Leonid Brezhnev at
the first summit meeting in May 1972. Yet it is a fact
that the main Soviet effort to prepare the Syrian and
Egyptian armies for war actually took place after the
signing of the "Basic Principles." In believing that Moscow would live up to the American understanding of
detente, both Americans and Israelis opened themselves
to surprise by the Arab attack. This false interpretation of
the Soviet view of detente prejudiced the evaluation of
evidence right up to the day war broke out in October.
Subsequent Soviet behavior also exposed detente as a
snare when taken uncritically by intelligence estimators
and policymakers.

It is a matter of record that Moscow did not inform
the United States of impending hostilities and did nothing
to stop them while the Arabs appeared to be at least
temporarily in the ascendancy. On the contrary, it tried
to extend the conflict while urging the Arab oil producers
to use oil as an additional weapon against the West. Only

after the Israeli counteroffensive was well under way did the Soviets show interest in a cease-fire. They obtained this by threatening to intervene directly and "end" detente. To avoid this possibility, Washington exerted intense pressure on Israel. In successive moves, during and after the war, a cease-fire halted the Israeli advance, permitted the reprovision of the encircled Egyptian Third Army and introduced the United Nations Emergency Force along the Israeli-Egyptian front.

Soviet broadcasts in Arabic presented all these moves as part of a concerted maneuver to consolidate and expand neocolonialist positions. Other broadcasts attacked the elements alleged to be undermining the Soviet-Arab front against Israel and reminded Arabs of their dependence on Soviet aid.

While allowing the Americans to induce Israeli withdrawals, termed "disengagement pacts," Moscow also hedged against a peace endangering its ambitions by drawing closer to Syria and the Palestine Liberation Organization. In the course of intense American efforts for a Syrian-Israeli disengagement, concluded in May 1974, Soviet obstruction took the form of Foreign Minister Gromyko's sudden appearance in Damascus during the final stages of negotiations. The immediate result of his appearance was a hardening of Syria's demand for a linkage between disengagement and complete Israeli withdrawal from captured territories. While the Syrians eventually gave in on this issue, their insistence on excluding paramilitary actions from the cease-fire was sustained. This gave the PLO—and therefore the Syrians—license to resume hostilities at will. Instead of seeing Soviet obstructionism for what it was, American analysts uncritically accepted the argument that its actions were no more than an attempt to gain equality with the United States in the process of negotiation. Dismissed was the evidence that any settlement—either to create a genuinely peaceful situation or even merely to lessen the level of arms supplies—is perceived by Moscow as inimical to its ambitions for dominance in the Middle East.

Despite the weighty evidence of Soviet obstruction before, during and since the Yom Kippur War, American policymakers continue to cling to their expectations of a constructive Soviet role in the settlement process. Dismissing the most formidable effort to overturn the regional balance, these analysts still find it fashionable to proclaim Moscow's goal as nothing more than winning formal acknowledgment of its role in the region. Precisely what this role might be is not defined, but the implication is that a definitive settlement would be an acceptable means for achieving that goal. Such faulty analysis reflects a consistent failure to discern the magnitude of Soviet involvement in Middle East politics, diplomacy and warfare. The record is one of chronic understatement and miscalculation regarding both the extent of Soviet capabilities and their degree of interest in controlling Middle East oil flows, in base rights and defense pacts and in direct involvement in hostilities and obstruction of the diplomatic process.

American policymakers and their advisors, largely as a result of accepting the misleading abstraction of detente as a working premise—even before it became established as a formal American objective—have failed to achieve a full and rational understanding of the Soviet role in political processes under way in the region. In a variety of subtle and self-deceiving ways, commentators have gone to great pains to highlight problems confronting Soviet policymakers—thereby giving exaggerated emphasis to presumptions of caution, restraint and responsible behavior. At no point was the Arab-Israel conflict understood as the growing fissure it represents in the foundation of world politics: a Soviet challenge to the balance of power. Thus at critical junctures in this conflict throughout the 1967–73 period, Soviet objectives, policies and intentions were perceived either as opportunistic or speculative—but not as the inexorable outcome of a genuine campaign with major investments of resources and prestige, involving the deliberate assumption of major risks.

So it is that after three decades of cold war, coexistence and detente, there remains an abject American failure to recognize that the principal Soviet interest in the Middle East is to exploit the region's endemic tensions in order to promote its own global strategic objectives. Such incessant miscalculation conforms to a pattern of defeatism which confuses reality with the comforting illusion that if the Kremlin is not cooperative, it is at least not destructive.

III

THE DEVOLUTION
OF
UNITED STATES
POLICY

THE containment policy launched by the United States in 1947 was born of a direct and growing Soviet threat to Europe. Britain's economic exhaustion and discouragement left the United States no alternative but to become involved in the eastern Mediterranean again for the defense of Europe. Nevertheless, the present American decline in the Middle East is rooted in the failure to perceive regional conflict and tension—systematically exploited by the Soviet Union—in the broader context of European security.

One need only note the forthright manner in which the United States reacted to the crises in Greece, Turkey and Iran on the one hand and the indecisive and ambiguous American reaction to the first Arab-Israeli war of 1948–1949 on the other, thus setting a sorry pattern for the future. Neither the United States nor Europe would adequately perceive Soviet initiatives in the Arab lands as a direct threat to their mutual security interests. At least they weren't to act as if they did.

The Dulles policy launched in 1953 was shaped in the cold war context with the objective of containing Soviet power, largely by creating military pacts. Rather than commit American troops to the area, the United States would help her friends with economic and military aid. Accordingly, the Turco-Pakistani agreement was signed in April 1954, and in the following two months Washington concluded military aid agreements with Iraq and Pakistan.

Urged on by the United States, the British signed the Suez evacuation agreement in October 1954. Under its terms, Britain would vacate the base by 18 June 1956 and each party would pledge itself to uphold the 1888 Constantinople Convention maintaining free passage through the canal for the ships of all nations. But it was not Britain's intention to surrender its paramount power in the region.

In order to offset this loss, London's client, Iraq, was encouraged to conclude a mutual assistance pact with Turkey on 19 February 1955. The pact was declared open to all members of the Arab League and to any other state interested in the peace and security of the area. Britain joined in April 1955, Pakistan in September and Iran in October. Known as the Baghdad Pact, it was designed to strengthen the so-called "northern tier" of Middle East defense against Russia.

While containment of the Soviet Union has always

been our primary objective, successive American administrations attempting to achieve this goal did not realize
the importance of engaging American prestige in an
all-out effort to terminate the Arab-Israeli conflict. From
the establishment of Israel in 1948 until the Suez-Sinai
War of 1956, American policy followed a narrow interpretation of the Tripartite Declaration of 25 May 1950
limiting the sale of United States, British and French
armaments to the Middle East. American policymakers
preferred to leave the day-to-day management of the
region's problems in the hands of Britain and France
because of their predominant interests in the Middle East.
Our failure to redress the arms balance upset by the
Soviet-Egyptian arms deal in 1955 helped prepare the
way for Israel's participation in the Suez-Sinai imbroglio
of October 1956. At the height of the crisis, Prime Minister
Anthony Eden of Britain, correctly realizing what was
at stake, cabled President Eisenhower on 6 September
saying, "If our assessment is correct and the only alternative to military intervention is to allow Nasser's plans
quietly to develop until this country and all Western
Europe are held to ransom by Egypt acting at Russia's
behest, it seems our duty is plain. We have many times
led Europe in the fight for freedom. It would be an ignoble
end to our long history if we accepted to perish by
degrees."[1]

Unfortunately the United States, against its own real
interests, opposed the Anglo-French action and saved
Egypt's Nasser.

Two months later the Eisenhower Doctrine was promul-
gated, promising American intervention to assist any Middle Eastern country threatened with Communist inspired

aggression. The American interest in the region was clarified in terms of its strategic and economic importance to the free world and the need to prevent Soviet domination over it.

Nevertheless, the local conflict was derogated to marginal importance despite growing indications that Moscow had embarked on a policy of systematic exploitation in the Arab-Israeli zone. In a series of arms deals, Moscow provided weapons and equipment in quantities that were bound to provoke an explosion sooner or later.

The Suez-Sinai debacle of 1956 and its indirect consequence, the Iraqi revolution in July 1958, were turning points in the rethinking of the region's security relationships. Pressure from Washington, supported by Soviet threats, compelled London and Paris to abandon their plan for the seizure of the canal. Anglo-French prestige virtually disappeared, while at the same time that of the Soviets gained considerably with minimum risk and cost.

Clearly, Britain and France could no longer act independently in defense of their vital interests if such actions led to war and conflicted with the policies of the two superpowers. By abruptly terminating the Anglo-French security plan for the region, the United States found itself with the role of primary defender of common Western interests in the Arab-Israeli zone. This development transformed a multipower rivalry into the more inherently unstable bipolar Soviet-American competition for political influence and strategic advantage.

Seeking to outflank American efforts at containment, the Soviets supported Nasser's pan-Arab and anti-Israel policies. They correctly assumed that tension and instability would undermine the Western influence which

was paramount in the region, and would therefore promote their objectives. Soviet interests thus coincided with
those of Nasser, who was out to undermine the moderate
pro-Western regimes for reasons of his own rather than
as a conscious tool of Soviet imperialism. Similarly, Nasser's militancy, bordering on brinksmanship vis-à-vis Israel,
stemmed also from the need to assert his leadership in
the Arab world, whether or not this served as the Kremlin's weapon against American influence.

The American response was reduced to the defensive
one of reacting and containing, while leaving the initiative
to the Soviets and their clients. The attempt to organize
strength in the area collapsed in July 1958 with the down-
fall of the monarchy in Iraq. The revolt was viewed
against the backdrop of armed rebellion in pro-Western
Lebanon beginning in May 1958 and was thus seen as
threatening the collapse of Western influence in the
Arab East.[2]

The Lebanese crisis consisted both of outside intervention on the part of Egypt and Syria—then merged as
the United Arab Republic (UAR)—and the domestic issue
of whether Lebanon's president should succeed himself
in office. With the infiltration of men and supplies through
Syria in support of Muslim forces, and with the Lebanese
army adopting a neutral stand, the struggle became truly
partisan along Muslim-Christian lines and threatened to
end in favor of the UAR, then dominated by Egypt.

Indeed this possibility became a reality on 14 July,
after the unexpected Iraqi revolution abolished the monarchy. Not a few observers saw the lightninglike coup
as an Egyptian-Soviet conspiracy carrying the incipient
threat of a comparable coup in Jordan, resulting in Soviet

domination of the Middle East. Citing the Eisenhower Doctrine, Lebanon issued the call for United States intervention. Accordingly, to preserve the regional balance, the first United States Marine units landed unopposed on the shores of Beirut.[3] Simultaneously, a Marine combat unit from Okinawa moved into the Persian Gulf. An airborne battle group from Germany and a Composite Air Strike Force (CASF) from the United States arrived at Adana, Turkey. The Strategic Air Command assumed an increased alert status, and the Sixth Fleet concentrated in the eastern Mediterranean. In conjunction with these moves, Turkish troops began to concentrate on Iraq's borders, and two days later, on 17 July, British paratroopers landed in Jordan at the invitation of King Hussein.

Although the nature, scope and timing of the military moves into Lebanon and Jordan suggested possible intervention in Iraq, Washington and London hesitated. Large-scale Soviet maneuvers on the frontiers of Turkey and Iran, an impressive airlift staged from Odessa on the Black Sea to Bulgaria, and diplomatic and propaganda efforts against "American aggression" served to induce restraint by posing the possibility of Soviet intervention.

Only subsequently was it learned that Moscow had had no intention of intervening on behalf of Iraq.[4] Washington had declined to use King Hussein's claim to the title of chief of the Arab Union of Iraq and Jordan as a reason to intervene. Yet, unlike the Suez-Sinai war 22 months earlier, the rapid buildup of powerful land, sea and air forces in the eastern Mediterranean was an impressive demonstration of how military and political action may complement and reinforce one another in limited war or crisis diplomacy. The fact nevertheless remained that the American effort to unite the Arabs into an anti-Communist pact came to an end with the downfall of the monarchy in Iraq.

In the early sixties, the United States turned to the general theme that economic development, whether the recipients were military allies or not, provided the best means for stabilizing the region and countering Soviet influence. The threat was no longer seen in conventional military terms but rather in terms of subversion and "wars of national liberation." Indeed, given the newly acquired Soviet second-strike capability, the East-West contest centered on gaining supremacy in the Third World. The rules of engagement were now confined to the indirect strategy of undermining the opponent through the instruments of trade, economic and military aid, limited intervention and war by proxy. While the countervailing forces of nationalism and unstable regimes denied the Soviets a decisive breakthrough in the Third World, they did not prevent the significant spread of Soviet influence, especially in the Middle East and Africa.

But the pattern of American response to the Soviet challenge lacked sophistication. It followed the line of least resistance and tended to take an exaggerated view of aid dollars as an instrument of policy. Thus, at a time when moderately pro-Western regimes such as Jordan, Lebanon, Saudi Arabia and Tunisia were recipients of assistance, including some military equipment, successive United States administrations directed repeated offers of aid also to the radicals led by Nasser's Egypt. The heavy American food assistance program carried out in Egypt, at the same time that country was receiving both military and economic aid from Moscow, was a symbol of this policy.

The policy backfired, since Nasser continued to focus less on the development of Egypt and more on efforts to expand his influence in the Arab world—notably in Yemen. Repeated attempts at courting Nasser were explained as a means of "keeping a foot in the door" or of providing Egypt with an option so as to prevent it from falling entirely into the Soviet orbit. This philosophy was especially prominent during the Kennedy administration, when overtures to "nonaligned" states were numerous and a further impetus was given to unsuccessful attempts at establishing a rapport with Egypt.

Looking back at United States policy in the decade preceding the Six Day War in 1967, it seems that American credibility eroded because short-term interests were served at the expense of long-term objectives. The 1958 revolution in Iraq demonstrated the limits of attempting to control forces in the area, just as the attempt to promote economic development did not arrest the growth of Soviet influence. Those states that were willing to pay a price for their alignment with Washington were repeatedly placed on the defensive because their "nonaligned" adversaries were accorded benevolent treatment by the Americans. The radicals, on the other hand, were able to enjoy Soviet political and economic assistance, ride the crest of the wave of radicalism, become the midwife to a new force in the Third World and at the same time gloat over economic assistance from the United States.

Support for this policy was justified along the following lines: the "moderate," conservative regimes, many of which were either monarchies or sheikhdoms, were weak, while the radical, militant republics were "forward looking" and aggressive. Overt and strong American identification with the conservative regimes would therefore alienate the radicals. It was only a matter of time before the monarchies would be overthrown and then the United States would find itself without support throughout the entire region. Moreover, if Washington engaged too much of its prestige in support of the moderates, then under attack by the radicals, it would incur the risk of an unnecessary confrontation with Moscow.

Nowhere was this policy more discredited than during the Yemen conflict of 1962 to 1967. In the ensuing stalemate, what had begun as a civil war threatened to spill over into Aden and Southern Arabia, to jeopardize the internal stability of Saudi Arabia and to increase the risk of a pro-Egyptian coup in Amman—which in turn might trigger a clash with Israel. Such was the possible chain of consequences that led from Yemen to Jerusalem.

Yet, the State Department played into Egyptian hands. The United States hoped to avert escalation by exchanging recognition of the republican regime for a withdrawal of Egyptian forces.[5] Despite denials, Washington sought to condone Egyptian intervention as the price for a peaceful settlement that would result in an Egyptian withdrawal. But the much sought "phased withdrawal" cut no ice with the Egyptians. When the policy failed, the United States strove for containment through inaction, on the assumption that since Egypt lacked the physical resources for protracted war it would sooner or later disengage of its own accord. Throughout this entire period, Washington failed to reduce its aid program to Egypt in spite of strong Saudi protests. At the same time, recognition of the republicans in Yemen had eliminated the possibility of any constructive negotiations with the royalists to seek a compromise between the two factions. Ironically, the royalists proved to be very much alive in the end.

Washington failed to draw the obvious conclusions from the Yemen debacle. The new Kennedy administration also attempted to establish its "New Frontier" credentials in the Middle East by using the Yemen affair as an example. Since it was trying to demonstrate that the Soviets were not the only champions of social change and progress, where better to make the point than in the archaic, theocratic Yemen, whose Imam had surprised everyone by dying in his bed? And besides, was it not a golden opportunity to prove American friendship to Nasser's Egypt and wean both him and the entire radical camp in the Arab world away from the Soviet orbit? Needless to say, not one of the radical Arab or African or Asian states let up in their attacks on the United States as the "imperialist" enemy of progress.

These very elements bring the Suez-Sinai imbroglio of 1956 to mind. On that occasion it was assumed that American opposition to the tripartite invasion of Egypt would identify the United States to the entire developing world as anticolonialist and particularly as siding with the anti-Israeli sentiments of the Arab world. By saving Nasser, it was thought the United States would dramatically demonstrate its stand against aggression and for Arab nationalism. It was thought that such a display would be adequate to safeguard the strategic and economic interests of the West. There was enough in this formula—which Dulles lived to regret—to satisfy both idealists and realists.

However, unlike the Suez Crisis of 1956, the Egyptian offensive in the Yemen with Soviet supplied arms now appeared to call not for condemning aggression but for condoning it. American acquiescence in Egyptian aggression would, so it was thought, finally bring about that elusive alignment with Arab nationalism. This was in fact the same motive as that which guided us in our condemnation of the British, French and Israelis in 1956. The decision adopted by the Kennedy administration to recognize the Yemeni republic implied acceptance of the destruction of the Yemeni Imamate, even if it threatened Saudi Arabia and British power in the Arabian Peninsula.

This policy had a clear impact on Soviet actions in the region and on the attitudes of local powers. The conservative regimes in need of American assistance to withstand subversion realized that identifying with the United States would label them as "imperialist lackeys" and thereby provoke even greater pressure. Some, like Saudi Arabia, sought to alleviate the pressure by adopting extreme positions on other issues, particularly the Arab-Israeli conflict, hoping thus to win a degree of respectability and acceptance in the Arab context. Others, like Morocco, Lebanon and Tunisia, established formal relations with Moscow, hoping that a controlled relationship would secure them an entrance ticket to the "nonaligned" camp. At the same time, the Baathists in Syria and Iraq tried to outdo Nasser by adopting an even more militant Arab stance. Taken together, these trends clearly did not favor the American position and contributed to the erosion of its credibility and diminished influence.

The Six Day War of June 1967 marked a turning point in the development of United States relationships with the Middle East. While in some respects it represented the culmination of past mistakes, in others it was the opening of a new chapter dominated by the Arab-Israeli conflict—an issue policymakers had hitherto tried to evade. It was a culmination in the sense that Nasser would not have challenged Israel's deterrent capability in the series of moves he made in the second half of May 1967 had the United States adopted a more resolute policy against him while supporting the conservatives. A more determined and overt support for Jordan's King Hussein might have prevented him from making his abrupt turnabout on 30 May, when he aligned with Egypt.

Along with American indecision whether to break the blockade imposed by Nasser on Israel's southern port of Eilat, Hussein's decision contributed to the feeling of encirclement by Israel—and to its final decision to strike at Egypt. Further, a more openly deterrent posture vis-à-vis the Soviet Union might have tempered—if not prevented—Soviet opportunism in provoking the conflict by deliberately misleading Egyptian intelligence about an impending Israeli attack on Syria. Bad judgment in execution of American policy again turned out to be a factor that contributed further toward unsettling the situation.

Israel's victory and the Soviet-American diplomatic exchanges that followed produced a reordering of priorities in American policy. Top priority was given to the prevention of another outbreak of hostilities because of the fear of a Soviet-American confrontation. Next perceived was the need to prevent Soviet attempts at hegemony by forcing superpower polarization in the Arab-Israeli conflict.

Decision making designed to further these priorities left

much to be desired, and some mistakes can already be identified as causes of subsequent American setbacks.

In the first instance, because Israel's victory was so decisive and Arab pride so hurt, the State Department believed the United States should refrain from close identification with Israel. But because Israel was universally perceived as a protegé of the United States, the attempt to appear distant from Israel was regarded by Arab governments as rather insincere.

Second, although it was the Soviet-sponsored regimes of Egypt and Syria and not the oil-producing states that suffered defeat, the State Department preferred to encourage Arab solidarity with Nasser rather than split the Arab states and strengthen the conservatives. This approach played into the hands of Cairo and Moscow. Since Nasser was working for a break in relations between Washington and all Arab states, the American overtures to him were used by Egypt as an instrument of pressure against the conservatives and proof that the United States considered Nasser the key to the Arab world.

An American statement of support for Israel after the war, but not necessarily for all of Israel's territorial conquests, coupled with a strong affirmation of friendship with the conservative Arab regimes, might have been a more rewarding approach. Instead, spokesmen for the administration, including President Johnson, sought to appear neutral and stressed their readiness to help in the peacemaking process. The Arabs, nevertheless, saw such American pronouncements as equivocation and therefore saw no compelling need to negotiate a binding peace.

Nasser was thus encouraged to pursue further his policy of uniting the Arab world under his leadership, using the conflict with Israel and Soviet support as levers. Moscow meanwhile launched both an intensive rearmament program for Egypt and Syria and a diplomatic offensive aimed at opening new doors to its influence.

Washington, for its part, unwittingly abetted this policy by placing a 135-day embargo on arms supplies to Israel, which lasted until the beginning of 1968.

Nasser's success in convening a summit conference of Arab leaders in Khartoum in August of 1967 was in itself a demonstration of America's failure to prevent polarization along the lines of the Arab-Israeli conflict. The hard-line Arab decisions at Khartoum were meant to serve as yet another platform for a Soviet-Arab political and diplomatic offensive to remove United States presence and influence from the region. It was used to mount additional pressure on Israel, to energize the Soviet-Egyptian diplomatic offensive and to maintain a high level of tension.

The change of administration in Washington did not bring about a change of strategy. Tactics continued to be determined solely by events and the need to respond to them. A case in point was the Nixon decision, in February 1969, to embark on a course of multilateral diplomacy for the purpose of achieving a comprehensive settlement of the Arab-Israeli conflict. It failed to reflect realities and it mistook tactics for strategy.

Israel was clearly the dominant military power in the area, and it was aligned with the United States in the eyes of both the Soviets and the Arabs. The Soviet over-tures to Washington, at the end of 1968 and early 1969, for superpower negotiations on the Middle East were a transparent ploy. A more cautionary approach might have

considered the possibility that the Soviets sought to
maneuver the United States into returning Israeli-held
territories to Moscow's Arab allies, with all the tactical
military advantages these territories represent, without
having to pay the price of peace. From this perspective,
the Soviets can be seen to have had a number of objectives:
first, to unite the Arab world against America and Israel;
second, to increase pressure on the West for an imposed
solution on Arab terms and to isolate America in support
of Israel; then, to isolate Israel from America; and finally,
to achieve the coercion of Israel into accepting all or most
Arab demands. If successful, such a program would greatly
enhance Soviet prestige in Arab eyes and would also
reinforce Moscow's presence in the region.

United States policymakers should surely have known
that in a contest with the Soviets on the definition of a
peace settlement, Washington could never outbid the
Soviets in their support of the Arab positions. Worse still,
until the 1967 war the Kremlin had not addressed itself
to the question of whether Israel could be militarily overcome by its Arab neighbors. But Washington's position
after the war—that America was committed only to Israel
proper, and not to its 1967 conquests—itself created a
"gray" zone and an opening for greater Soviet military
involvement on the side of the Arabs.

The Soviet expectation was that its military support
of the Arabs no longer risked confrontation with the
United States if Moscow now emphasized that it had
no design—direct or indirect—against Israel if defined
by its borders before June 1967. The Soviets understood
that this outward position could be changed later.

The Soviet strategy of splitting the United States and

Israel coincided with an American decision, early in the Nixon administration, to negotiate with the Soviet Union on the whole range of issues that had dominated the cold war era. In preparation for what later developed into the present detente policy, the Nixon administration adopted the concept of "linkage." This meant that the issues of Vietnam, the Middle East and arms limitation would no longer be treated as isolated topics in Soviet-American talks. All the issues would be test cases for detente, with progress on one creating some impact on the others. The choice fell first on the Middle East, perhaps because Nixon considered it a "powder keg."

Thus developed the Soviet-American bilateral talks of 1969. The contention by American officials that the Soviet-American talks were a means of exposing the true Soviet and Arab intentions and could do no harm was later proved to be mistaken. The more Washington gravitated toward "moderate" Arab demands the more Moscow moved still further toward extreme Arab demands. In its desire to put distance between itself and Israel and between Moscow and the Arabs, Washington itself went a long way in these talks toward satisfying the Arab demand for total Israeli withdrawal.

In November 1969, Secretary of State William Rogers put forward a proposal that any settlement of the territorial dispute arising out of the 1967 fighting should be based on Israeli withdrawal from the occupied territories—except for "insubstantial alterations" of the prewar boundaries. Precisely what was meant by that phrase was unclear, but Washington's pronouncement of the general nature of a settlement in advance of negotiations was a gratuitous concession. Moreover, rather than being called

upon to effect a peace treaty that would include guide-
lines for diplomatic and commercial relations, the parties
were required only to declare a "cessation of belligerency"
and deposit mutually signed "contractual" papers with
the United Nations or the great powers. This formula,
subsequently termed the "Rogers Plan," prejudged the
extent of the territorial alterations that would constitute
defensible borders as required by Resolution 242. It also
diminished Israel's bargaining position and encouraged
the Arabs to adopt a rigid rather than flexible position.
The Soviets responded by aligning themselves even more
closely with the Arab position and further escalated their
military and political support of Egypt.

Early in April 1969, Nasser had repudiated the cease-
fire agreement and formally launched his war of attrition.
The Egyptian position had moved a long way from the
passive refusal to implement U.N. Security Council
Resolution 242 of 22 November 1967.* To this day,
the Soviet-Egyptian interpretation of this resolution always includes three key demands reflecting a common
doctrine against a lasting peace. First, every joint Soviet-
Egyptian communique demands an Israeli withdrawal to
the vulnerable armistice lines, now designated as "secure"
boundaries. Second, Israel must now agree to a Palestinian
state. Prior to October 1973 the demand was for a mass
influx of Palestinian Arabs within Israel's armistice frontiers. Third, reference continued to be made to a "political
solution," not to a final peace or to an explicit sovereign
recognition between the parties. The need to preserve
the roots of the conflict is as much a Soviet prerequisite

* See Appendix.

as it is an Egyptian demand. Nowhere is peace between Israel and the Arabs mentioned as the ultimate object of Soviet-Egyptian diplomacy. Whenever the words "peace" or "peaceful settlement" are used, they are employed in very general and abstract terms, applied never to Israel but to "the Middle East." Indeed, at no point during Soviet-American discussions in 1969 did Moscow consider, propose or accept any initiative truly consistent with the intent of Resolution 242—that is, favoring direct Arab-Israeli negotiations on all aspects of the conflict and leading to mutual recognition within secure and recognized borders. By the time the United States had realized the failure of its efforts, Nasser had accelerated his war of attrition in a bid to supply a note of urgency to the superpower dialogue.

With the escalation of hostilities in 1970, American credibility was harmed as it became evident that the Rogers formula for a settlement antagonized both sides. While it did not go far enough to satisfy Arab demands, it managed to compromise vital Israeli security interests and to undermine her negotiating posture. The nature of these aborted talks and the tension that rose between Washington and Jerusalem also served to encourage Soviet opportunism—which threatened relations between the superpowers themselves.

In August 1970 a cease-fire was finally signed ending Nasser's ill-fated war of attrition. He and the Russians were surprised to discover that their combined military efforts could not wrest air superiority over Suez from the Israelis. In fact, the Israeli Air Force had proved its superiority even over the Soviet force in Egypt by downing five of its pilots in a single engagement. They had been actively participating in operations against Israel.

What the Soviets and Egyptians could not accomplish by force of arms they were able to achieve through brazen violation of agreements. It is a sorry commentary on the American politics of defeat that these adversaries could count on a lack of American resolve to cement their gains. The cease-fire signed on 7 August 1970 stipulated explicitly that the Soviet-manned surface-to-air missile belt was not to be moved toward the canal. This point had been the parry in the Suez fighting because any violation of it would inevitably have nullified Israeli air superiority over the canal, thus allowing for an Egyptian crossover. On the very day of signature, under cover of darkness, the Soviets and Egyptians moved their missile belt right up to the canal. Israel protested to America, but the United States presumably was not able to substantiate this claim until several weeks later. Jerusalem's hand was stayed by arguments that "peace was at hand" and should not be dissipated by "precipitous" action. Upon American corroboration of the violations, the United States had achieved a pyrrhic victory. The price of this "achievement" of American policy was paid three years later with Egypt's successful crossing of the canal in the Yom Kippur War under cover of the strategically located SAM missile belt.

Sadat learned from Nasser's mistakes. Instead of exclusive reliance on the Soviets and on the military option, he set out to win American support away from Israel by a series of military and political strokes. First, he removed the suffocating Soviet presence, then he prepared for total war with limited objectives and with full Soviet support. Finally, he followed this with political action—again with limited objectives, but this time with American support.

The Yom Kippur War of October 1973 highlighted two new expressions of the American politics of defeat in the Middle East. Despite the fact that the concerted Arab invasion on two fronts, in the Sinai and on the Golan Heights, was a blatant act of aggression encouraged by the Soviets and resulted in serious losses for Israel in the war's first days, the American resupply of sorely needed equipment did not come until the eighth day of the war. Presumably, the policy was to let Israel bleed enough so as to make her more amenable to American manipulation. What a lesson for our allies!

This lesson with regard to the true face of American policy was brought home again to Israel and to the American public when, toward the end of the war, our government threatened to airdrop water, food and medical supplies directly to the encircled Egyptian Third Army should Israel not agree to permit such resupply by Egypt. Here the concrete American policy objective was to save the defeated aggressor, Sadat, from the sobering humiliation of surrendering his army to the victims of aggression. Events are proving that American enforcement of political defeat upon the military victor has prepared the fertile ground for the next even greater conflagration in the Middle East—with the added danger of miscalculation by all parties.

In the aftermath of the Yom Kippur War, three basic factors conditioned the new environment: the severe Israeli intelligence blunder together with the Israeli failure to push the Egyptians back across the Suez Canal; American involvement toward the end of the fighting, which saved Egypt's encircled Third Army and thus secured for the United States a dubious role in postwar political action; and the consequent Arab, especially Egyptian, conviction that the United States could be pressed into extracting further concessions from Israel.

This new atmosphere permitted Washington to increase the distance it had placed between itself and Israel. This policy was facilitated by the American decision to prevent a devastating Israeli victory and resulted from American weakness in the face of an Arab embargo.

Instead of exploiting Israel's military power in order to demonstrate to the Arabs the vulnerability of their oil as a weapon, the Nixon-Ford administration preferred to support a shift in the regional balance that was bound to lead to the conclusion that America saw its true interests in the region lying with Arab oil and money. Thus were laid the seeds of a future war.

Washington's belief, however, was that the change in United States policy in 1973 was a triumph of American strength and firmness. Unlike the preceding six years, when poor relations with the Arab states stemmed from an ambivalent posture, the decisive American intervention in the 1973 war was seen as enhancing American-Arab relations. American firmness and resolution in applying pressure on Israel is considered to have persuaded the Arabs that the United States alone wields effective influence in the region.

Ironically, the success of the Israelis in battle, using American weapons, enhanced the reputation of American patronage among Arabs. The Soviets, in the absence of any kind of leverage on Israel that is comparable to American influence, were unable to offer anything beyond arms. However, the test of arms now became secondary to the competition in moving Israel to concessions, and here the United States easily won the contest. However hopeful the United States may be that the world will accept its perception of its role in the Middle East, it is the reality of the differing Arab perception which will govern the evolution of events. America is perceived in the Middle East today by most Arabs and many Israelis as searching for a graceful way to disown Israel. The buzz-words in this policy are: "American, Soviet, and United Nations guarantees."

Policymakers did not fail to compliment themselves when in January 1974 the first of three "disengagement pacts" was concluded. The entrapped Egyptian forces were released, the Israeli threat to Cairo was removed and the Suez Canal was to be reopened. Moscow was to regain the short water route from its Black Sea ports and Mediterranean positions to project its formidable naval presence around the Arabian peninsula. Renewed and speedier access thus would enhance Moscow's worldwide naval flexibility.

Four months later, another "disengagement pact" was concluded, this time with Syria. Difficulties here derived from the fact that there was much less give on Israel's northern front than in the south. Unlike the Sinai desert, separating the Israeli Negev from the Suez Canal, the Golan Heights are more obviously valuable to Israel's security.

Secretary Kissinger's third shuttle mission—an attempt to win a Sinai II pact—collapsed in late March 1975. President Sadat had overbid his hand and doomed the talks. Apparently encouraged by American reverses in Cambodia and Vietnam, Sadat took a hard line, demanding effective control of the Sinai passes and refusing practical or even verbal steps toward peace with Israel.

Henry Kissinger reacted with well-publicized tears and a less publicized—but more effective—six-month campaign to undermine the position of Israel and its leadership. On the plane back to the United States, a "senior official" opined that Israel had been short-sighted to turn down the Egyptian offer. Within days after his return, Kissinger began ostentatiously receiving analysts with impeccable credentials of even-handedness to offer "opinions" on the future direction of American Middle East policy. King Hussein of Jordan was feted at a red-carpet reception in Washington while a trip planned by Prime Minister Rabin was postponed, pending the outcome of what had become known as the "reassessment."

More insidiously, Kissinger and President Ford ordered that arms shipments to Israel be cut off. Gradually but inexorably, Israel found itself receiving excuses instead of aircraft, tanks, artillery and support systems. This obstructionism did not fully abate until spring 1976. Reacting to this and other attacks stage-managed by Kissinger, notably snipings in the press and on Capitol Hill, seventy-six senators wrote President Ford and called for secure and recognized boundaries for Israel, direct negotiations and meaningful steps toward peace and reconciliation. The letter also referred to the "special relationship" between the United States and Israel and termed as "dangerous" the cutoff of arms supplies.

The letter was partly successful; it acted as a partial check on what was becoming an increasingly perverse policy. But throughout the summer, Kissinger's pressure on Israel continued. On 1 September, it resulted in the initiative of the Sinai II* pact. There were some significant differences between the Sinai II agreement and the draft which had proved unacceptable in March. But these were primarily military differences in the Egyptian view. Substantially, there were almost no Egyptian political accommodations toward Israel.

The effects of the Sinai II pact and the reassessment which led to it were several. First, Israeli dependence on the United States and the Rabin government's obsession with that dependence had become a semi-institutionalized part of American-Israeli relations. Second, the ability of the United States to coerce Israel was demonstrated, and pondered, by the United States, Israel and the Arab states. Third, an old Arab canard—that America could ultimately be relied upon to dictate to its "agent" Israel—was given positive reinforcement. Fourth, the Soviet policy of pushing the Arabs to push the United States to push Israel was vindicated. Fifth, any chance of transforming the step-by-step approach into a mechanism of Arab-Israeli compromise and conciliation died. Sadat asserted that he had not made a pact with Israel but only with the United States. Finally, Secretary Kissinger's policy of expedience, brute force and duplicity was shown to be facile but effective.

The reassessment, Kissinger said, ended when Israel signed the Sinai II pact. But its lessons still remain valid to this day, vitiating Israel's political independence, hardening Arab revanchism, encouraging American amorality and fostering "godfather" politics.

These American achievements are clearly tenuous and

* Known also as Interim Agreement.

short-lived. The Arab-American rapprochement is based on the false premise that Arab hunger for American-delivered Israeli concessions is satiable. Arab expectations are higher than anything the United States is capable of delivering. What is certain is that despite the resumption of American relations with Cairo and Damascus and of Arab protestations of moderation tailored for public opinion, the causes of the Arab-Israeli conflict remain unresolved. If anything, ongoing Arab attempts to expel Israel from every world forum are in direct proportion to American efforts at "even-handedness." Finally, Soviet mischief-making remains unchecked. As of this writing, the Soviets have redeployed in Iraq and Libya. Moscow waits patiently on the sidelines for Syria and Egypt to wring the last Israeli concession out of America, at which point considerations of war can be reactivated with the promise of immediate Soviet resupply of those Arab states involved in the confrontation.

IV
ISRAEL AND CONCEPTS OF NATIONAL SECURITY

A^N ambiguous symbol at best, the term "national security" is even less comprehensible than usual in the political lexicon of the Middle East because of the conflict and tension endemic to the region. This condition is traceable largely to the sectarian and fragmented nature of Middle East society and the failure of the region to regain its political equilibrium following the demise of the Ottoman Empire. Chronic instability, manifested in subversion, revolution and communal tensions, intertwines with border problems. Such instability becomes even more complex when entangled in great power rivalries. Concepts of security, therefore, remain a matter of subjective evaluation or pure speculation, depending on one's view of the interplay between the relative strength of local regimes and vicissitudes of international politics.

Unlike its Arab neighbors, Israel regards national security to be synonymous with survival. Consequently, security is the fundamental determinant of Israel's foreign policy.

This perception evolved after 1949, when the inability to make progress in improving relations with Arab neighbors became manifest. For despite Israel's poor geostrategic position following the 1948–49 war, its expectation was that a formal peace settlement would quickly follow the armistice agreements. However, the collective refusal of the Arab states to reach any accommodation permitted the conflict to fester and become further entangled in inter-Arab and great power rivalries, thereby rendering any settlement even more remote.

It was one thing to convince Washington and Moscow to suspend their cold war and work together against the British on the Palestine issue and another matter for Israel to attempt a course of nonalignment.[1] More significantly, toward the end of 1952 Moscow embarked on a course of anti-Semitic agitation, accusing leading Czechoslovak Communists of working with Zionists and Americans. In all the Soviet bloc countries, attacks on Israel became regular and virulent. The tentative policy of nonalignment collapsed and Israel naturally gravitated toward the West. The Kremlin was relatively quick to realize that under normal security conditions, Israel's ethnic and democratic ties to America were too powerful to permit her being used as a bridgehead against continued Western interests in the region.

After the 1955 Czech arms sale to Egypt, Israel asked the three Western powers for equipment to counterbalance the new Egyptian weapons. The United States declined to sell Israel any arms. Britain urged Israel to make territorial and other concessions to the Arabs in order to avert war. France also refused and confined itself to an unsuccessful attempt at persuading Nasser not to transfer his obsolete arms to Algeria. All sides concluded that the Tripartite Declaration had gone by the board.

The Czech arms sale and a strident Arabism that daily grew stronger turned Nasser into an all-Arab hero, an image used to isolate Iraq and prevent the accession of Syria and Jordan to the Baghdad Pact. At the same time, Egypt's hardened line took the added form of extreme verbal attack and mounting terrorist raids deep inside Israel.

If anything, the Egyptian shift from apparent moderation to the mobilization of resources for an assault on Israel underlined the new realities of local and global power politics in the region. The general situation deteriorated with the repercussions that followed Nikita Khrushchev's statement on the Middle East to the Supreme Soviet on 29 December 1955. After expressing his sympathy for Jordan in her opposition to the Baghdad Pact, the Soviet leader launched a virulent attack on Israel. This new policy toward Israel was welcomed on 1 January 1956 by a spokesman of the Arab League in Cairo, who noted that the Arabs could now count on Moscow's moral and material support in their dispute with Israel.

There followed a recurrence of incidents on the Egyptian and Syrian borders in January, resulting in a United Nations Security Council condemnation of Israel for its retaliatory raids. More ominous in Israeli eyes was a

British-sponsored Security Council resolution from which the members had deleted a reference to a "mutually agreed solution" to the Palestine problem. Israel's policy of moderation had failed, and on 17 June Moshe Sharett formally resigned, after having been foreign minister for eight years. He was succeeded by Israel's former ambassador to the Soviet Union, Golda Meir. Renewed incidents on the Jordanian border and the Egyptian nationalization of the Suez Canal on 26 July dashed any hopes for calm in the region.

Although increasingly concerned for their security, the Israelis were not eager to become allies of the former colonial powers in an attack on Egypt. For Britain, cooperation with Israel was repugnant because of all the hopes it still harbored for the Arab League. Nevertheless, collusion was far more attractive for Israel than continued isolation. The marriage broker between Britain and Israel in this case was France.

Though similar in general purpose, the objectives of Britain, France and Israel were hardly identical in the Sinai-Suez War of 1956. For the British and French, securing freedom of traffic in the canal was the common and positive objective. However, the British hoped to reaffirm their position in the region with or without Egypt's Nasser, while the French considered his deposition the *sine qua non* for a solution to their Algerian dilemma.[2]

From Israel's perspective, the high priority given in the Anglo-French plan to destroy the Egyptian Air Force would protect Israel's populated areas from Soviet-built Ilyushin aircraft. The operation would also permit the destruction of the Arab terrorist bases in Gaza—then under the direction of the Egyptian General Staff—the destruction of the Egyptian military before it assimilated the new Soviet equipment and the opening of the Gulf of Aqaba to Israeli shipping as an alternative to the Suez Canal.

These plans implied large-scale ground operations in the Sinai desert and command of the air. Unless the potentially powerful Egyptian Air Force was destroyed before the major ground offensive in Sinai began, Israel would neither commit her infantry nor expose her populated center to possible attack by Soviet-built Egyptian bombers.[3]

Accordingly, in the secret meetings held at Sèvre from 23 to 25 October to coordinate Anglo-French and Israeli plans, Ben-Gurion sought confirmation that the Egyptian Air Force would be destroyed before the major ground offensive began. With major Israeli production and population centers only eight jet-flight minutes away from the nearest enemy base, he also sought aerial surveillance of Egyptian airfields from the moment Israel crossed the frontier. In the tough bargaining that ensued, Britain agreed to begin bombing Egyptian airfields 36 hours after the beginning of the Israeli offensive. With aircraft based on Cyprus, France would provide fighter cover for Israeli cities and paradrops of food, ammunition and trucks to the advancing Israelis. Only after receiving assurances of indispensable air cover did the Israelis consent to co-ordinated action with the British and French. Thus, operations Musketeer (Anglo-French) and Kadesh (Israeli) became interdependent parts of a carefully orchestrated diplomatic ultimatum. The anticipated hostile response from Egypt would permit the neutralization of the Egyptian Air Force, an Israeli thrust into the Sinai and an Anglo-French occupation of the Suez Canal Zone.

Despite the military victory in the Sinai campaign—which contrasted with the poor showing of the Anglo-French operation—Israel was in no position to dictate a settlement. The opportunity to reach a settlement was lost primarily because of American pressure and failure to insist on a peace settlement. Compelled by Washington to withdraw from Sinai, Israel was granted three conditions which were to ensure her security: the promise by Egypt to refrain from hostile action; Egyptian consent to United Nations Emergency Forces along the Gaza Strip, at a few points on the Sinai-Negev frontier and at the entrance to the Gulf of Aqaba; and a promise by the maritime nations to secure free navigation through the Tiran Straits.

In the absence of any explicit guarantees either by the United Nations or the great powers, Israel unilaterally declared that a blockade of the Tiran Straits would be considered as cause for war. Egypt, however, reaffirmed the state of belligerency but stated she would refrain from attacking Israel until and unless assured of victory. Once again, the United States had all too easily given up the possibility for real peace implicit in Israel's victories on the ground. Instead, we were assured of greater and more devastating conflict in the future.

After 1957, the Israelis developed their military strength and evolved new concepts of war and defense. Their doctrine in the years following the Sinai campaign excluded a purely defensive strategy and emphasized offensive operations having as their object the destruction of the enemy's forces. Major battles would take place only on enemy soil. For both military and political reasons a war would have to be short and decisive.

Strategically, the doctrine meant that in case of war, the Israel Defense Forces would not be dispersed and tied down to defensive positions. Rather, the emphasis would be on concentrating superior strength against one opponent before turning against another. Tactically, the offensive implied reliance on mobility, speed, coordination and surprise. Only the superior quality of Israel's man-power could, up to a point, nullify the effect of Arab numerical superiority.

In putting such a doctrine into practice, Israel had to consider a number of conditions: First, unlike its opponents, Israel had to develop the ability to switch its forces rapidly from one front to another. Second, tactics had to be such as to make a quick victory over one's opponent feasible; this implied speed, shock and mobility, not massive firepower. Consequently, emphasis was placed on the development of armored formations and their over-head support, the Air Force. The result was a completely mobile, flexible military instrument unified under a single command and capable of delivering lightning blows and switching rapidly from one front to another.

Israel's dramatic victories in June 1967 were a military triumph due largely to the successful execution of the above doctrine. Adhering to the classical principles of war—surprise, flexibility, concentration of power, economy of effort, intelligence, planning and training—the Israeli Air Force within three hours demolished Egyptian air power, thereby altering the relationship of forces in the Middle East. In the ensuing 127 hours, Israel smashed the Jordanian and Syrian air forces, destroyed a four-nation military alliance, conquered territories nearly six times her size and severely damaged Soviet prestige.[4]

While the Sinai campaign of 1956 had been won only over Egypt, Israel won the Six Day War over Egypt, Jordan and Syria. Whereas the Sinai war was limited in objectives, as well as the area, time and the forces involved, the 1967 fighting was greater in scope. For this war Israel tapped all its economic, industrial, scientific and manpower reservoirs.

With the success of its concentrated air strike, the outcome turned on the ability of the United States to deter Soviet intervention and the speed with which the Israel Defense Forces could rout the combined Arab armies before international diplomacy secured an unconditional cease-fire.

Foremost among the manifold results of the war, Israel acquired strategic advantages that she had lacked beforehand. Her new borders on the banks of the Suez, the Jordan River and the Golan Heights provided effective security in depth and, so long as Israel was half alert, provided an ideal defense against conventional aggression. The surprise Egyptian and Syrian attacks of 1973 only confirm the military significance of such depth.

Strategically, the Six Day War reversed Israel's previous relationship with Egypt. Occupation of the Sinai not only removed the threat of rapid junction between Egyptian and Jordanian forces across the Negev desert, but put Tel Aviv 300 miles from the Egyptian forces—while Cairo was now only 80 miles from Israeli armed forces. Air bases in the north of Israel fell out of Egyptian combat-aircraft range, while corresponding Egyptian bases came into easier range of the Israeli Air Force.

Important Egyptian population centers and industrial complexes were now also more vulnerable to Israeli attack.

Actual or potential air bases in Sinai gave Israeli combat planes 15 minutes more time than they had before the war and deprived Egyptian planes of comparable margins. Moreover, the easier striking range implied a faster turn-around and larger payloads for attacking aircraft, not to mention increased alternative bases.

Similarly, conquest of the Golan Heights reversed the prewar strategic relationship with Syria. Control of these heights removed the long-standing threat to a score of villages, gave Israel complete control of the Jordan River headwaters and placed the Israel Defense Forces within 40 miles of Damascus. In like manner, Jordan's loss of the West Bank denied her a critical base of operations against Israel. Israeli troops were now within 25 miles of Amman and in a stronger position to threaten Mafraq and Samakh—Jordan's main links to Syria and Iraq.

The fact that Israel was caught sleeping in October 1973 has led to considerable controversy over what constitutes a truly secure peace. All sides concede the necessity for revising Israel's strategic doctrine. The issues, however, cut across the spectrum of party platforms, political and economic institutions, military structure and community life. Opinions range from the doctrines of "elastic defense" to "secure borders," all of which are intrinsically related to the equally divergent Arab and Israeli perceptions of great power interests and rivalries in the region.[5]

On the one side, the concept of "elastic defense," as employed in the 1967 conflict, implies a mobile armed force, a flexible defense structure, a strategy based on offensive operations and a willingness to concede territory in border negotiations. On the other side, the doctrine of "secure borders," employed after the 1967 conflict, most conspicuously at the Bar-Lev line on the Suez front, implies a more sizeable but static armed force deployed in border defense, an increased emphasis on mass fire-power, a strategy based on conventional land warfare with the ability to absorb a first strike and a resolution to acquire and maintain as much border territory as possible.

Critics of the "secure borders" option claim that it was the reason for the initial heavy Israeli losses in the October War, that the strain on the Israeli economy would eventually be prohibitive and that such a doctrine would encourage Arab governments to escalate qualitatively their foreign weapons acquisition. A posture of "elastic defense," on the other hand, is criticized in that it destabilizes an already volatile situation by virtue of its reliance on offensive action and that such a doctrine might permit Israel to be pressured into excessive territorial concessions to Arab states in border negotiations prior to a genuine peace settlement.

The debate on the nature of Israel's security needs goes on outside of Israel as well. It is instructive to note the sanctimonious casuistry which often characterizes this "nonpartisan" debate on secure boundaries in the Arab-Israeli zone. Using as their rationale that there is no absolute security—as though life were a matter of absolutes—such theorists in America join the Soviet-Arab demand for a complete Israeli withdrawal from the territories taken in 1967. This demand is itself an indication of Soviet-Arab success in transposing the issue of territories as the cause rather than a symptom of the conflict. It rests on the deceptive argument that security is not a function of territory. Dismissed in the Israeli case is the fact that an increase of relative security may have an absolute value in the event of a life-or-death battle. It is one thing for us to belittle the strategic and tactical roles of territory where the security of a foreign state is concerned. After all, our lives are not the lives directly on the line. It is, however, quite another thing for us to realize that we jeopardize *American* security by flippant talk of guaranteeing and securing Israel without sufficient defensive depth on the ground. It is this lapse in a rational appraisal of our strategic interests in the region which is one of the principal causes of our current politics of defeat in the Middle East.

It is admittedly sometimes hard to remember the old dictum of power politics: any diminution in the concrete strength on the ground of an ally or other guaranteed power—such as, for example, Czechoslovakia in 1938— only increases by a dangerous factor the propensity of an enemy power to test that guarantee. When the test comes, it comes not for the purpose of grabbing the brass ring, but of taking over the entire merry-go-round. Like security, territory is not an absolute. It is, however, a valuable tool for hammering out a true and lasting peace. Its meaning should not be lost in the fog of complacent thought.

V

ARMS AND
THE ARABS

AT a time when the southeastern flank of NATO is threatened by a continued Soviet military buildup as well as by instability in the Arab and Greek-Turkish zones other disturbing trends in American policy merit attention.

While modest arms deals with Saudi Arabia have been a long-standing feature of American policy, current efforts are underway to extend this policy to Egypt, Syria and Iraq. The opening move in this trend was made in February 1976, with the sale of six C-130 transport planes to Egypt.[1] An attempt at a similar sale to Syria failed. However, the L-100 aircraft, the civilian version of the C-130, was sold to both Syria and Iraq.

Far more significant was the determination with which

the Ford administration moved to secure Congressional approval for the sale to Saudi Arabia of sophisticated missiles. Contemplated for eventual approval in piecemeal fashion was the sale of 2,000 Sidewinder AIM 9-J air-to-air missiles, 2,500 Maverick air-to-surface missiles (supplementing an earlier sale of 1,000 then in the pipeline), 1,800 TOW antitank missiles and an unspecified number of laser-guided bombs.[2] At the time, only the proposal to sell 2,000 Sidewinders was under active consideration. However, after the true magnitude of this series of projected sales was revealed on 1 August 1976, Congress created a storm.

On the day following that revelation, the Senate Foreign Relations Committee released a staff report on arms to Iran.[3] It cited that in May 1972, during a stopover in Iran, President Nixon made the secret decision to "let Iran buy anything it wanted" in conventional American weaponry. The Committee report also revealed that since then the United States had supplied Iran with more than $10 billion worth of weapons, from supersonic aircraft and Spruance class destroyers to the Hawk air-defense missile systems, antitank missiles and helicopters. Almost immediately, the Iranian sales were studied in the context of the sales proposal pending with Saudi Arabia. In addition, the Pentagon was eager to supply Jordan with a sophisticated $540 million air-defense system to be paid for by the Saudis. Kuwait was also a beneficiary of American military largesse.

Embarrassing questions were raised. Does America gain by spurring the arms race between Iran and Saudi Arabia? Is it wise to provide Jordan with greater capabilities against Israel—America's asset in the Middle East? Should

America accept the role of being the largest supplier of arms in the world, selling as much as the Soviet Union and all other nations combined? Why were the normal procedures for policy review within the Pentagon suspended? No answers to these questions have been forthcoming. Even the casual observer can now point to the grim spectacle of the United States having become a major supplier to both sides in both of the Middle East military rivalries—between Arabs and Israelis and between Iran and the Arab states bordering the Persian Gulf.

Nevertheless, on 1 September 1976 the Administration officially notified Congress of its intention to provide Saudi Arabia with a compromise proposal of $700 million in weapons, military construction and training. The sale, subsequently approved after the initial requests were substantially modified, included 650 Mavericks, 850 Sidewinders and 1,000 TOW missiles. While significantly lower than the 1,500 Mavericks and 2,000 Sidewinders originally sought, the latest deals brought the total planned arms sales and military construction for Saudi Arabia to more than $7.5 billion in 1976 alone.

Due to these and other sales there is now a growing threat to the regional balance in the Middle East. The current arms sales to the area reflect a short-sighted tendency to rely on military equipment in the pursuit of foreign policy goals. This tendency has had a destabilizing effect by fanning regional arms races. The argument that arms sales and aid abroad permit the United States to expand its political influence in the recipient countries is highly exaggerated. Both Iraq and Libya were the recipients of significant amounts of American military aid when they had conservative monarchies. Their regimes are anti-American today. The most likely effect of military assistance, if its recipient is nondemocratic, is simply the destruction of the fibre of the society we are supposedly aiding. In the past three years alone, an estimated $12 billion in arms supplies have been delivered by East and West to the Arab countries. Another $10 to $12 billion in arms and military facilities have been contracted for delivery beginning in 1977. Saudi Arabia alone is getting $9.5 billion in arms and military construction from the United States.

There is no sound military reason for America to sell Saudi Arabia the Maverick, Sidewinder and TOW missiles.[4] On the contrary, the combination of the Maverick air-to-surface missile and F-5E aircraft converts that fighter into a bomber. The Saudis have 100 F-5Es. Theoretically, this system will be deployed only against Iraq and South Yemen. But it could well be deployed against Israel. The obvious target is Eilat, a town of 20,000 inhabitants. A few dozen Mavericks could incapacitate the port facilities and the oil pipelines from Eilat to central Israel. Several hundred Mavericks could kill thousands of Israeli civilians.

Moreover, it is probable that the Saudis would transfer the Maverick F/5 system to Egypt, Jordan or Syria. This would make Israel even more vulnerable to bombardment. Its magnitude can be deduced from the total number of Mavericks—some 1,650. In a crisis situation wouldn't Israel feel constrained to launch an offensive strike against these F/5s? At the same time does not possession of this system also increase the confidence of Arab leaders in their ability to undertake a first strike successfully? This is why the sale of such a system to Saudi Arabia increases the probability that an Arab-Israeli crisis will explode into an Arab-Israeli war.

Until the recent arms deal, the United States had approved some 200 TOWs and some 4,000 Dragon anti-tank missiles supposedly to guard against the very low probability of an Iraqi tank attack against Saudi Arabia. Now that another 1,000 TOWs have been approved, the probability is very high of their being transferred for use against Israeli tanks and armored personnel carriers.

Similarly, a reasonable argument can be made that Saudi Arabia requires a few air-to-air missiles for added insurance against the small probability of an Iraqi air attack. But the sale of an additional 850 Sidewinders, supplementing 300 already approved, now means a high probability of their being transferred for use against Israeli aircraft. There can be little doubt that the emphasis on enormous quantities of air-to-air and air-to-surface missiles is designed by Saudi Arabia as a response to Israeli air power and as a means of establishing an offensive capability against Israeli cities. Given Israel's dependence on control of the air in order to overcome its numerical disadvantage elsewhere, the new missile capability in Arab hands is of potentially decisive importance.[5]

At a minimum, Israel will request compensating equipment. Thus, in escalating the weapons race, American arms deliveries to the Arabs undermine this country's own diplomatic initiatives. Such weaponry in Arab hands encourages a false sense of power and an unwillingness to make the kinds of concessions necessary for peace. The Arabs are not threatened by Israel and can use the enormous supplies of arms now being received from both

East and West only for aggression against Israel. It is the Israeli, not the Arab, sense of security that must be bolstered.

The presumptions underlying these arms sales are fallacious. Contrary to prevailing wisdom, Israel does not retain an indefinite qualitative superiority over its neighbors. The implication that Israel does not really need additional weaponry to offset supplies to the Arab states is simply not correct. Similarly, the presumption that Arabs are incapable of assimilating sophisticated military technology was proved grossly wrong in the 1973 fighting. Therefore, the implication that there is no harm in selling Arabs anything and everything is manifestly wrong.

No less faulty is the presumption that the Saudis and Kuwaitis will not transfer American weaponry to the confrontation states. The better presumption is that if the Saudis did *not* transfer arms to the front-line states in the next war, they would by their own inaction detonate internal efforts to overthrow their feudal, theocratic regime. A Qaddafi Arabia is as likely as a Saudi Arabia. Indeed, this possibility has grown as Arabia's new military elites have become ever more fascinated with new sophisticated weaponry.

There is also the presumption that if the Maverick, TOW and Sidewinder were not sold, the Saudis could buy the same from other countries. While this might be true of some weapons, it is definitely not true of those systems. Nowhere can the equivalent of these sophisticated weapons be purchased. Their sale constitutes a radical departure in American policy and has produced risks and dangers to American interests that heavily out-

weigh perceived advantages. They represent a dubious
and irresponsible legacy passed on to the new administration.

Beyond the parameters of the Arab-Israeli conflict,
current arms transactions are triggering a whole chain
of "balancing" transactions in the Persian Gulf region—
especially by Iraq and Iran. The final outcome is uncertain, but the short-range result is for more instability
in a region of the world already dangerously unstable
as a result of the inherent vulnerability of autocratic
regimes.

Of another magnitude but no less disturbing are the
ongoing efforts originating in high intelligence circles to
portray Israel as an illegal exploiter of American technology to undermine American markets.[6] Israeli arms sales
abroad are highlighted as a threat to the American arms
industry, as though the United States is in an adversary
relationship with Israel. A few simple facts are in order.

Total annual world arms sales amount to approximately
$20 billion. Of this, the United States exports about $12
billion—making it the largest exporter in the world. Following the United States on the list of exporters are the
Soviet Union, France and England. Israel's total export
of military equipment is little more than $300 million,
of which $250 million is purely of a military nature; the
additional amount consists of equipment which is adapted
for civilian use. From these figures it is abundantly clear
that Israel accounts for no more than 1.5 percent of the
total world arms trade. Current attention focused on
Israel with respect to defense exports is out of all proportion to reality.

At a time when the United States is providing important economic aid to Israel, it is contradictory to restrict her potential for further economic growth and export expansion. We can't have it both ways with the taxpayer's money. Israeli exports of military equipment also assist the Israeli economy to maintain important defense industries—such as the Israeli aircraft industry. Such measures of selp-help lessen Israel's need to rely on the United States.

These transactions also aid the United States in a material sense. A substantial portion of the component parts in Israeli defense equipment is manufactured in the United States. These Israeli orders represent additional income for the United States, increase the job market here and assist in the recovery of the American economy. Many of these American components are sold by Israel in a modified form for relatively small markets which American industry might not be geared to satisfy, thus expanding the sale of such American components. For example, the General Electric J-79 engine may not be saleable in an American F-5 but may meet the needs of certain countries as a component in the Israeli *Kfir* fighter plane. In fact, we should be encouraging a program of Israeli foreign military sales because of its significant net benefit to the American economy.

The Israeli share in arms exports should therefore be seen in its proper context: not an attempt to compete with America's $12 billion annual sales of military equipment, but rather a heroic attempt to maintain and improve an economy forced to sustain a Soviet-inspired weapons race. It is an economic fact that no small country can maintain a modern defense industry designed purely for its own use. Moreover, it is only natural that given the combat-proved effectiveness of certain of Israel's custom-made weapons systems, many countries desire her equipment. Indeed, American defense manufacturers and security analysts received a steady flow of information from Israel on the performance and effectiveness of both American *and Soviet* equipment and parts used in the Yom Kippur War. This additional information has enabled American manufacturers to introduce critical improvements, thus making the American product more valuable to foreign countries. America has lost no soldiers in testing such weaponry under actual combat conditions.

Some defenders of the United States politics of defeat claim that Israeli foreign military sales must be restricted for the very purpose of making Israel ever more dependent on the United States. The end objective of such a policy is indeed to make Israel a burden, one which can be more readily shrugged off at the appropriate time.

Anti-Israel distortions are also prevalent with regard to American foreign military sales. The total value of foreign military sales for 1976 was $10.3 billion. Of this amount, as cited by the Defense Security Assistance Agency, Saudi Arabia led with more than $3 billion, Iran with more than $1.5 billion and Israel with $953 million. And while Israel can rely only on the United States, the Arab states can purchase from the Soviet Union, England and France. In such circumstances, Israel cannot be expected unilaterally to agree to a reduction in its arms. Until arms control is accepted not only by all Arab states but also by the external powers, Israel will be forced to rely on her own capacities to defend herself and also on the United States for economic and military assistance.

It should be abundantly clear at this point that arms sales to Israel give her the security with which to bolster her free and democratic institutions, especially since they are based entirely on an educated citizens' army. In the case of the Arab states, unfortunately, the opposite is true. The mad race on the part of American arms manufacturers to sell the Arabs anything and everything they desire is helping to convert what are basically feudal societies, as in Arabia, into regimes based increasingly on a military elite. This is the unavoidable outcome when arms are showered upon an illiterate people with no sense of participatory democracy. In fact, whatever chance our leaders might have had of seeing feudal Arab institutions evolve in time along democratic channels is being inexorably destroyed. In the case of the sundry more modern dictatorships in the Arab world, such an arms policy is only deepening the peoples' subjugation to military rule—however disguised in the trappings of parliamentary democracy.

VI

EGYPT AND
ARAB QUESTS
FOR
DOMINANCE

FOLLOWING the Egyptian revolution in July 1952, mounting American pressure finally succeeded in inducing a British military evacuation from the Suez Canal Zone. Under such circumstances, Nasser was both shocked and angered at the Turkish-Iraqi pact of February 1955 since it implied the continuation of a British strategic presence in the region, albeit under a new guise.

However, to Iraq's perennial Prime Minister Nuri Said, a modified British role was preferable to a sharpened Soviet-American contest for the region. The British treaty with Egypt in 1954 notwithstanding, Iraq's pact with Turkey in 1955 touched off a new and intense rivalry between Cairo and Baghdad for influence in Syria, Lebanon and Jordan. Whereas Nasser looked to the 1950 Arab League Collective Security Pact—involving Egypt, Iraq, Syria, Jordan, Lebanon, Libya and Saudi Arabia—as the effective substitute for the departing British, London and Washington wanted to strengthen the northern tier of states in opposition to the Soviet Union.

Nevertheless, what most rankled Nasser was not opposition to the inclusion of Turkey and Pakistan in Middle East defense planning—a Turkish-Egyptian alliance was then under active consideration—or a *de facto* arrangement with Britain and the United States; rather, Nasser was outraged by Western preference for Iraq over Egypt and by the implication that his arch rival in Arab affairs, Nuri Said, was more important, reliable and stable.[1]

The choice of Baghdad as the pivot of the alliance exacerbated Egyptian-Iraqi tensions and thereby facilitated Soviet penetration of the region. Moscow now cultivated the theme that the Western military alliances endangered the security of the Arab people since they carried the threat of Soviet retaliation. The Soviets also began to trade on the friction created by Egypt's rejection of American conditions for military aid. The announcement, therefore, of an agreement in September 1955—but actually concluded the previous February—providing for the barter of Czech weapons for Egyptian cotton undermined Western efforts to stabilize the region and heightened Arab-Israeli tension.[2]

The arms deal, the largest in the history of the Middle East at the time, constituted a direct challenge to the Tripartite Declaration of May 1950 whereby the United States, Britain and France sought to control the flow of weapons into the region. Moscow's move thus shattered the Declaration's balance-of-power principle and raised the continuing problem of just how far the West would go to redress the balance. With this stroke, the Soviets had "leapfrogged" the northern tier barrier and became a Middle East power in fact. At the same time, from 1954 to 1956, Nasser initiated terrorist attacks from the Gaza Strip against Israel—attacks which became a critical element in Israel's subsequent involvement in the Suez-Sinai war of October 1956.

With the removal of British influence from Egypt after the 1956 war, Cairo was able to increase its involvement in the politics of Arab nationalism and to display a greater freedom of action in the Arab East. Heretofore, traditional Egyptian geopolitical interests had centered on terminating the British military presence in the Suez Canal Zone, assuring for itself the waters of the Nile and union with the Sudan. Within this context, delineated by the resources of the Nile and the Red Sea, Egypt's Arab interests were secondary.

In the Arab East, the primary Egyptian objective was the avoidance of isolation in order to deny Syria or the Hashemite monarchies of Iraq and Jordan hegemony in the western Fertile Crescent and to minimize any prospect of potential Saudi hegemony in the Peninsula.[3] Nevertheless, Egypt's subsequent emphasis on Arabism marked a departure from the past and a serious beginning for its self-appointed role as the vanguard of the Arab nationalist struggle: the emancipation of all Arabs from Western influence and their eventual union under Cairo.

In the decade following, Nasser's policy of Arabism and "positive neutralism" grew. Egypt increased its involvement in the domestic politics of Arab states and assumed a more strident and aggressive role in pursuing its hegemonic ambitions in the Arab sphere. A principal manifestation of this was the establishment of the ill-fated union between Egypt and Syria in the context of the United Arab Republic, formed in 1958. Having encouraged the removal of Western presence from the Suez Canal Zone, America discovered to her surprise that she had facilitated Soviet-Egyptian intrigue and subversion not only within the region but also along its periphery.

In the context of Nasser's theory of Egypt's role in the Arab, African and Muslim spheres, Egypt tried to outflank the French base at Djibouti and the British base in Aden, which controlled the approaches to the Red Sea and the Suez Canal. This was done by closely coordinating tactics with the Soviets in support of insurgent movements in Southern Arabia and East Africa. The Western capability to introduce fleets into the Red Sea posed a potential threat to both Soviet and Egyptian expansionism. The southern gateway to the Suez Canal is the Bab al-Mandeb Strait, and its effective control could be used to deny access to the Western fleets. Freedom of action for Egypt required the removal of the British presence in Aden, which was the principal base for the protection of British oil interests in the Gulf, and the location of Britain's strategic reserves that could be deployed into East Africa and the Middle East.

Yet it was not until 1960, and in the wake of African independence, that Cairo projected its influence into sub-Saharan Africa. By then, Nasser's preoccupations inside the Arab circle and his successful penetration of the Fertile Crescent and Southern Arabia inspired

Cairo to reach for more than merely establishing Egypt as the leading power of the Nile and Red Sea.

Nevertheless, although Nasser's personal prestige was sufficient to mobilize pro-Arab sentiment, cohesive unity was another matter. When in February 1958 Egypt and Syria merged to form the United Arab Republic, pan-Arab sentiment reached its apogee, and a serious blow was struck at the Hashemite monarchy of Iraq. The end came on 14 July 1958, when the pro-Western government in Baghdad was overthrown and both the King and Prime Minister were murdered. The pivot on which the Baghdad Pact alliance had been centered was eliminated. Viewed in the broader context of the May outbreak of armed rebellion in Lebanon, the revolution in Iraq stimulated fears of a total collapse of Western influence in the region. Immediate attention centered on the threat of a comparable coup in Jordan and a final victory for the rebels in Lebanon.[4] Accordingly, both states now invoked the Eisenhower Doctrine requesting military assistance. British paratroopers were dispatched to Jordan and American troops landed in Lebanon.

The intervention had a salutory if limited effect.[5] Egypt had stimulated the Iraqi revolt, but partly because of Israel's deterrent presence, it could not control subsequent events. Indeed, the regime of Abdel Karim Kassem proved surprisingly uncooperative with Cairo and challenged Egyptian leadership in the region. Nasser quickly recognized this threat and sought to overthrow the Kassem government. A pro-Nasser coup was quickly squashed by Kassem with the aid of the local Communists—encouraged by Moscow.

The rivalry with Iraq sparked the first crisis in Arab-

Soviet relations, the issue focusing on the treatment of local Communists. Whereas Nasser jailed his Communists and periodically released them on the eve of some visit by a Soviet luminary, Kassem sought to use his Communists against other political factions. In the final analysis, Kassem failed to establish Iraq as the regional alternative to Egypt, and in the five years following his overthrow in 1963, no Iraqi regime was able to muster the internal control of the prerevolutionary days necessary to promote Iraqi preeminence in inter-Arab affairs.

At the same time, the Syro-Egyptian merger into the United Arab Republic progressively deteriorated, and Syria finally seceded from the union in September 1961. Egypt's drive for genuine regional hegemony thus failed, despite the fact that during the three and a half years of its union with Syria there was no external interference in this unique experiment with Arab unity. Again, Israel's presence as a geographic and military barrier limited Egypt's capacity to control Syria and prevented a military response to secession. Israel's role in this regard was not appreciated by senior American analysts who were still smarting under their earlier failure to abort the creation of the Jewish state.

American analysts continued to downgrade the evidence of Egypt's quest for an imperial role in the Middle East, even when they turned their gaze to the Arabian Peninsula. Isolated and on the defensive, Egypt's opportunity to regain the initiative came one year later with the revolution in theocratic Yemen. Success there, if aided by Egypt, would recapture the momentum for Cairo, stimulate an internal challenge to the leading conservative Saudi regime and perhaps offer Egypt direct access to

Aden and South Arabia. The extension of Cairo's influence into South Arabia would enhance Nasser's now tarnished image and bring closer the tempting oil prize in Saudi Arabia and the Gulf.

In what subsequently developed as a war by proxy with Saudi Arabia, Egypt badly miscalculated in its intelligence estimates prior to intervention. Cairo failed to evaluate correctly the possible fields of battle and the attitude of the local population. Unawareness of the pitfalls of protracted conflict was underlined by the speed of intervention, which had assumed a quick and decisive victory.

Even after it was clear that enough outside aid was going to the royalists at least to guarantee the possibility of a protracted war, the Egyptians failed to revise their goals or broaden their options for disengagement. The fighting thus followed the classic pattern of a large, well-equipped army attempting to subdue a mountain-based guerrilla force working in small units with primitive weapons. As it developed, the fighting centered in unfamiliar mountainous terrain, and the Egyptian army was unable, as expected, to force a decision before the first winter.

The conflict demonstrated the limits of Egyptian power and the dangers of miscalculation and overextension. Not only did the war go badly, but the Yemeni Republic politicians proved exceedingly difficult to get along with. It was yet another instance of an Egyptian drive for hegemony stumbling over intractable local problems.

As it turned out, Egypt could neither destroy the monarchy nor secure the republic. Nasser subsequently likened his position in the Yemen to that of the United

States in Vietnam: he could not win, nor could he withdraw without loss of prestige and credibility.

Despite the protracted stalemate, the emergence of a republican regime buttressed by a growing Egyptian military presence encouraged the Adeni nationalists against Britain. It was in the Saudi interest to thwart any linkup between revolutionary Yemen and the Egyptian supported Aden nationalists.

The matter was brought to a head in the aftermath of the Arab-Israeli war of June 1967. Egypt withdrew from Yemen, the British withdrew from Aden and the Saudis were allowed to pursue their interests in South Arabia. Yet the Yemen conflict demonstrated the manner in which the dynamics of inter-Arab rivalry led to exploitation of the Arab-Israeli confrontation. The interrelationship cannot be ignored. Because of the protracted strife in Yemen, Nasser sought to unite the Arabs under his leadership by again using the Arab-Israeli conflict as the means. In 1964 he initiated the first of the Arab summit meetings, designed to prevent Israeli use of the headwaters of the Jordan River, while organizing the Palestinians—this time into the Palestine Liberation Organization.

King Faisal of Saudi Arabia could also play the same game. His response to Nasser's renewed bid for leadership was to launch what became known as the Islamic Pact. All Muslim states, regardless of their internal political systems, would be brought together under the aegis of Mecca, supposedly against the "Israeli menace."

King Faisal's proposed solidarity conference never took place, but the sharpening of the Saudi-Egyptian rivalry encouraged a renewed military alliance between Egypt and Syria. This new pact was portrayed as a defensive alliance against Israel. Saudi Arabia, however, was as much a target because Cairo considered the Islamic Pact an American attempt to challenge Egyptian leadership. In this manner, Nasser's race with Faisal for Arab leadership led to a commitment to Syria which enhanced his reputation as the Arab champion against Israel. Consequently, when in mid-May 1967, Moscow fabricated charges that Israeli troops were massing to invade Syria, Egypt reacted in a rapid sequence of politico-military moves making full-scale hostilities inevitable. In the end, the Syrian-Egyptian alliance in fact became the mechanism for unleashing the Six Day War, shattering in its wake the structure of politics in the Middle East.

Despite the new strategic configuration after the 1967 Israeli victory, peace did not follow. The Soviets had instigated the war in the first place and now began to rearm Egypt to thwart any settlement. With the flow of Soviet weapons a constant source of encouragement, Egypt showed little inclination toward political settlement on any terms other than Israel's unconditional return to its prewar lines. The United States had forced Israel's withdrawal from Sinai in 1957 and might be induced to do so again.

On the diplomatic front, the United Nations Security Council passed Resolution 242 to *guide* negotiations for settlement. Whereas Israel correctly maintains that the resolution provides the basis for negotiations toward an overall settlement, Arab leaders, supported by Moscow, view the resolution as self-executing, erroneously requiring Israeli withdrawal from *all* occupied territories. Obviously, the Egyptians hoped that the Soviet Union would persuade the United States to repeat the procedures of 1957—

pressure on Israel to withdraw without a formal peace. In these circumstances, and in the absence of a better alternative, the Israelis dug in.

With the passage of time, particularly within the context of the intensive Egyptian artillery bombardment of Israeli positions on the east bank of the canal, beginning in the autumn of 1968 and in the following war of attrition from March 1969 to August 1970, "security," in the Israeli perception, became increasingly identified with the retention of territories. More from necessity than desire, the new lines were said to be vastly superior to the old ones. At the same time, Israeli strategic doctrine was ambiguous with regard to the proper role to be played by its Sinai defenses—whether they were meant to absorb or repel an Egyptian first strike. The notion of strategic depth was not fully reconciled with the continued emphasis on mobile and offensive weapons systems.

On the other hand, Egypt's perception of security since the Six Day War had been portrayed as synonymous with the retrieval of territories—including those lost by Syria and Jordan. With the emergence of the Arab-Israeli conflict as a burning problem after the Six Day War, a new issue divided the Arab states. This was the question of how to deal with what the Arabs termed the "elimination of the traces of aggression."

One group, led by Egypt, gave first priority to the return of territories lost in the 1967 war. A second group, basing its position on "ideological purity," contended that as the establishment of Israel was in itself a form of aggression, the Arabs should seek total confrontation until the original "1948 aggression" had been removed. This group consisted of states that were not directly involved in the confrontation and was led by Libya, Iraq and South Yemen. Syria tried to enjoy the best of both worlds by adopting a tough position on the ideological level, while conducting at times a more pragmatic approach on the practical level.

The division of the Arab world into two camps—"reactionary" and "progressive"—so pronounced in the early sixties lost much of its significance. Not that the division vanished completely. Rather, awareness of the ties created by common culture became a kind of undercurrent and provided implicit leverage power in the hands of "progressives" for extracting growing amounts of financial support from the rich "reactionaries."

At the end of 1971, more than a year after Nasser's demise, Egypt's credibility had reached an all-time low. However, in 1972 Egypt's Sadat forged new links with a number of Arab states which became allies in the wartime coalition of 1973. The innermost circle of this coalition comprised Egypt, Syria and Saudi Arabia. The latter was vital because of its financial backing for military preparations and its possession of the oil embargo weapon. For Syria, the coalition marked the end of an isolation which had existed since 1967. Jordan, excluded from this grouping, replaced Syria as the odd man out. The realignment marked the reemergence of Egypt as a central factor.

Egypt's war option crystallized gradually over this period and its actual strategy evolved by mid-1972. The Six Day War had worsened Egypt's economic plight. The Suez Canal was closed, Sinai oil was lost, and the decline of tourism intensified the deterioration. Despite aid from the Arab oil producers, Cairo had to promote additional austerity and fight rising unemployment. When commodity prices rose sharply in mid-1972, there was a deterioration in the country's balance of payments leading to the placing of a serious restriction on imports. Egypt's aggression in October 1973 must thus be seen in the context of economic stagnation and of Sadat's clear admission that Egypt faced either war or economic collapse. Beyond economics, the loss in Egyptian morale and political stability was seen by Sadat as an insufferable situation.

Instead of Nasser's "steamroller" strategy of war and a clamoring for action on all fronts, Sadat opted for a more coordinated approach. The resumption of hostilities would take the form of a surprise offensive instead of a war of attrition. Additionally, coordination with only one other Arab army—that of Syria—would permit him to succeed in the necessary dissimulation. The plan called for a diplomatic offensive vis-à-vis the United States, with the club of an oil embargo and the snare of a peace conference as the focus.

A man of determination but proved tactical flexibility, Sadat, ever since his assumption of power upon the death of Nasser in September 1970, has had as his foremost objective an Israeli return to the 1967 lines by one means or another. Far more than did his predecessor, Sadat focused on the United States to achieve his objective even as he moved on the parallel fronts of war and peace.

At least until the failure of his national security advisor Hafiz Ismail's mission to Washington in March of 1973, Sadat without recourse to war could have negotiated an agreement similar to that obtained in September 1975: a reopened canal and an Egyptian presence on the eastern bank. He rejected this proposal advanced by Israel at the end of 1970. On the other hand, Sadat's substitute proposal in February 1971 was unacceptable to Israel. In both cases, the main divergence was an Egyptian insistence that Israel undertake in advance to withdraw completely from Sinai. But the reopening of Suez was not Sadat's objective. Rather, the goal was to obtain a fixed schedule for total Israeli withdrawal—each stage of which was to be agreed within a specified period.

Sadat also wished to redeem Egyptian military honor on the battlefield, to restore the credibility lost by his failure to act in 1971 as the "year of decision" and to cut down his wealthy rivals who posed as crusaders: Qaddafi of Libya and Faisal of Saudi Arabia. Whereas the former demanded immediate, integral union with Egypt, the latter began to brandish the oil embargo weapon as the most potent instrument in bringing Israel to terms.

Sadat had discarded the earlier hope of creating a powerful Egyptian-led bloc in the region through union with Syria, Sudan and Libya. Neither Syria nor Sudan was enthusiastic, and the wild rhetoric and erratic conduct of Libya's Qaddafi convinced Sadat that too close an association with him would be as dangerous as the proverbial ride on a tiger. Instead, Sadat turned eastward to the conservative and oil-rich states of Saudi Arabia and the Gulf sheikhdoms.[6] But a price was extracted. Qaddafi was to remain isolated in inter-Arab affairs, King Hussein was to be readmitted to the family of Arab nations and King Faisal was to decide how and when the oil weapon would be used. In return, Faisal agreed to apply immediate pressure on the United States as an earnest expression of his intentions. The objective was to evoke increased American attention and high-level intervention in the Arab-Israeli conflict. To many observers, the new Sadat-Faisal alignment and the restoration of Syrian and Egyptian ties with Jordan seemed promising. However, observers underestimated Sadat's capacity for duplicity. Sadat had also convinced Faisal that without the unifying force of war, the oil weapon would be ineffective.

The international psychosis that had developed around the problem of energy provided an excellent guise for winning strategic military surprise. Presumably, the confrontation had moved from the battlefield to the oil field. The credible threat of an oil squeeze was to speak for itself. Observers now believed that Sadat had concluded that Moscow was more interested in detente with the West than in a military operation against Israel and that he would therefore disengage from the Soviet Union. No less seductive was the widespread belief that Sadat would move the Egyptian economy toward capitalism and domestic reconstruction rather than war.

Meanwhile, behind the cover of peace rhetoric and an unusual calm on the Israel-Syrian front, Syrian-Egyptian coordination of war preparations intensified. Even Egypt's Foreign Minister Mohammed al-Zayyat, then amid an intensive diplomatic campaign in world capitals, was kept in the dark—to be used as an innocent source of deception.[7]

Despite strategic surprise, massive weaponry and political support from the Soviet Union, the Syrian-Egyptian onslaught of October 1973 was checked on the third day in the north and on the fifth day in the south.

The Arabs had planned their offensives to ensure that Israel could not reverse the advances before international political forces intervened. More specifically, Egyptian strategy combined the strategic offensive with tactically defensive operations. By crossing the length of the canal, Israeli air power was dissipated, and since no major operations were launched from the narrow bridgeheads, there was little room for the Israel Defense Forces to exercise their superiority in a war of maneuver. Nevertheless, once Israel had fully mobilized she was able to outmaneuver the Egyptians and achieve a surprise countercrossing of the canal. Only the pressure from Washington saved the encircled Egyptian Third Army from total disaster.

Today, Anwar Sadat's demands upon Israel remain what they were prior to the October 1973 aggression: an Israeli timetable for total withdrawal from the territories captured in the 1967 war. A new demand was now added for the creation of a separate Palestinian state for the West Bank and the Gaza Strip. Presumably, Egypt then would agree only to terminate the state of belligerency, not conclude a peace treaty. Ignored is the 1951 Security Council ruling that the armistice agreements of 1949 established a legal regime of "nonbelligerency" which was to last until the parties made peace.[8] Although the Arabs could not legally claim belligerent rights nor bar the Suez Canal to Israeli shipping, they offer no more today than what was conceded in 1949. Such is the state of progress.

Not even seasoned commentators fully recognize Sadat's extraordinary capacity for political survival or his agility in the beguiling arts of bluff, blackmail and deception that pass for diplomacy. His measure of success is marked by the extent to which practitioners of statecraft are unwittingly seduced into transposing cause with symptom, confusing reality with illusion and believing that movement alone constitutes progress.

Nevertheless, despite a qualified success in effecting Israeli withdrawals from Sinai, Sadat still finds the need to associate the survival of his regime with the concept of Egyptian national security. Such is the nature of our problems with any dictatorial authority. Unable to resolve the old dilemma of overpopulation and undercapitalization, Sadat is threatened from the left and the right. Aside from the Palestinians associated with the "rejectionist front," the junior officers within the army comprise another source of serious discontent. Not informed that they stared defeat in the face in 1973, this group resents the diplomats for being "slow" to exploit the "gains" they won for Egypt.

Civilian opposition is based on continuing poverty and the inability of agricultural output to keep pace with the population growth. "Hero of the crossing, where is our breakfast?"—a slogan of alarming food riots—shows how things are. Shortage of staple foods is endemic and inflation is rampant. People constantly line up in frustration for many essentials of life. Food riots occur from time to time. The new "fat cats," a crust of millionaire speculators in quick currency transactions and real estate deals, provoke envy, and the controlled press even calls for their "slaughter." The situation has become so bad as to penetrate even American media and is being reported by correspondents who have all along promoted the Washington celebration of Sadat's Egypt.

Sanguine expectations of enormous American and Western aid meanwhile put a damper on frustrations. But it is quite impossible politically for Egypt's needs to be met, and this will surely become apparent sometime in the not too distant future. The American taxpayer cannot be expected to accept what is tantamount to double taxation on the part of Arab states—one hand paying off Arabia for its oil and the other sustaining an ever-increasing dole for Egypt. American policymakers have attempted to ignore this political reality in their efforts to buy oil and the illusion of peace from the Arabs.

Saudi Arabia will pay for arms—but not food. Increasingly one hears voices in Egypt—even Sadat's on occasion—reminding the oil super-rich in Arabia that Egyptian blood in "October" has made their fabulous fortunes possible. Unless the Saudis move actually to share their wealth with Egypt—and this is equally incredible—the latter is probably headed for a collision with them as the profiteers of Egyptian "bloodletting."

While Sadat has been unable to make his case successfully with the conservative monarchy of Saudi Arabia, he fared worse with his more radical wartime ally, Syria. Damascus interpreted the Sinai disengagement incorporated in Sinai II as having taken Egypt out of the military equation—thus leaving Israel free to mass its strength against Syria. A shift of the political center of gravity away from Cairo took the form of Syrian overtures to Jordan and intervention in the civil war in Lebanon. For the first time in a decade Damascus emerged capable of an independent initiative in changing the overall configuration of Arab alignments.[9] Syria's objective was to carve out an area of exclusive influence covering the region known as "Greater Syria," embracing Lebanon and Jordan and including domination of the PLO, the would-be representatives of Palestine. This undertaking was highly focused in both the geographic and political sense. It aimed not at the formation of a constitutional union, but rather at the creation of an exclusive sphere of influence—a protectorate. Sinai II was the occasion for Syria to put Egypt on the defensive by charging that Sadat had secretly colluded with Israel and the United States. President Assad of Syria was determined to out-maneuver Egypt in his bid for dominance in the Arab East. By January 1976, he boasted that Jordan was firmly aligned with Damascus, that the PLO was on the verge of being maneuvered into dependence and that a *pax Syriana* was a near certainty in Lebanon. By alternately or simultaneously supporting Christian and Muslim factions in the civil war, Syria gained the ascendancy in Lebanon. But the Muslim-PLO alliance opposed the political reforms advocated by Damascus. Their insistence on the total defeat of the Christians—on wholly upsetting the balance of social forces—ran counter to Syria's interest in holding the balance between the warring sides. Damascus understood that it had a better chance of creating an effective dependency out of ravaged Lebanon by supporting and subsequently *protecting* the isolated Christians rather than by adding to the ascendancy of the faction-ridden Muslim and PLO forces in that country.

In March of 1976 the cease-fire in Lebanon collapsed, and fighting escalated on all fronts with heavier weapons than at any time before. Syria's tactical maneuvers against the radical and PLO forces brought about a new combination of groupings to oppose Syria. Libya, Egypt and

Iraq found common ground in sponsoring one or the other of the anti-Syrian factions in Lebanon. Just as Egypt had previously decided not to be derailed by Syria from the course charted in the Sinai agreement, so Syria was now determined to avoid a Muslim victory in Lebanon that might lead to effective partition and Israeli intervention. Thus, on 1 June 1976, the Syrian army intervened openly in Lebanon for the first time. Since then Syria has repeatedly maintained that its army will stay so long as the Lebanese authorities request it.

The incursion of Syrian troops into Lebanon raises the question of a "red line" beyond which Israel would be unable to accept any advance by Syria into the territory of Lebanon. This line was proclaimed in early 1976, but its precise location has never been specified. It is understood to carry both military and geographical connotations that may shift with changing circumstances. At no time has any Israeli spokesman defined the red line, but Israel's attitude toward developments in Lebanon continues to be dictated by security interests. The fact that Israel has not intervened—despite continued reference to a "red line"—can only be ascribed to American pressure.

What has in fact transpired in the Lebanese tragedy is that the United States has traded acquiescence in Syrian domination of that country for Syrian cooperation in the peaceful negotiation of Israel's retreat to the lines of 1967. The attempt to trade one country—Lebanon—for an agreement to accept concessions from another—Israel—will only facilitate the loss of both. Future historians would marvel at the native capacity of America as a supposedly Christian country to sell out Christian Lebanon to Arab Muslim ambition as part and parcel of the momentum to undermine the security of a Jewish state. The real issue in Lebanon was and remains a basic contest for sectarian-religious domination of the region. This contest has been partially dissimulated as a "rightist-leftist" struggle, with the help of uninformed Western journalists who actually believe what they are told in the Middle East.

It is good that the fighting in Lebanon has subsided. It is heartening that the ancient and proud Christian communities of that country have not been destroyed in a Muslim power grab. It is satisfying that Baathist Syria is finally the one applying its heavy hand to the various factions of the PLO in Lebanon and restricting their operations. It is, however, troubling that only a small number of American analysts of the situation have the courage to identify publicly the really serious dangers to Israel and American security interests. These dangers are implicit in Syria's moves regardless of whether its forces in Lebanon are 8 miles from the Israeli border or 80 miles. With time, Lebanon will surely become an additional confrontation state in the more than 50-year Arab war against the Jewish presence in Palestine. This will be true even if Lebanon is used only for the staging and movement of Syrian and Arab forces against Israel on a theatre of war which has been inactive for 29 years. Any serious student of the Middle East must ponder the proposition that the dream of recreating "Greater Syria," and progressively uniting the Arab world under its banner, is now within the grasp of Damascus in Lebanon. It must also be recognized that a triumphant Damascus may have its appetite whetted for the completion of its design to recreate "Greater Syria" by including Jordan

and Israel. In fact the temporarily sufferable existence
of Israel might even be considered a plus in such a
Syrian design because Israel can be counted on to block
Egyptian forces from directly countering a Syrian advance into a subverted Jordan. All this of course will
depend on whether Syria can continue to count on the
United States to restrain Israel's military hand, unwittingly, of course, against our own best interests. The Soviets
meanwhile are waiting patiently for the next stage in
the undermining of our security assets in the region.

The Lebanese experience has led to a realignment of
policies between Egypt and Syria, now cemented by
Arabian petrodollars. Those who had presumed to find
the Arab confrontation states divided over their strategy
vis-à-vis Israel have proved lacking in perception. Syria
has proved on the ground that she is master of a potential
new confrontation state against Israel and that she is
as productive as Sadat's Egypt in manipulating the United
States government to undermine Western interests in
the region.

VII

PERSIAN GULF RIVALRIES IN MOSCOW'S EQUATION

WHEN not engaged in confrontation with Israel, inter-Arab and Arab-Iranian rivalries emerge as the dominant theme in the areas contiguous to the Persian Gulf.

In Saudi Arabia, the traditional insular perception of security was altered by events in Yemen and Southern Arabia in the 1962–67 period.[1] But even before Nasser failed to recognize his dream of hegemony, the major Saudi task was to ensure that no united Yemen came into existence. United, the two Yemens would have a population more than twice that of Saudi Arabia, and if oil were ever discovered, the southwestern part of Arabia would become an important factor in the politics of the peninsula. Moreover, if the regime in Aden were to change, there could well be important support in the southern parts of North Yemen for breaking away from Sana and joining with a moderate regime in Aden. The possibility is not remote considering that many of the old South Yemen politicians, particularly those from the South Arabian League and FLOSY* who are now living in North Yemen, would like to return to Aden and establish a new regime. While some would be more "traditional" than others in their form of rule, most would espouse a united Yemen policy and would certainly attempt to win over the southern part of North Yemen. In that event, Saudi Arabia would cease supporting these leaders and would instead vigorously oppose them. Here one must note the persistent and widespread belief in North Yemen that the Saudis will one day seek direct access to the Indian Ocean by making a territorial claim on the Hadhramout area. Any sign promising unification of the two Yemens would prompt such a claim in order to outflank any union.

As for the United Arab Emirates, they could not alone resist an attack by either Saudi Arabia or Iran. Formerly known as the Trucial States, the newly formed UAE is comprised of the seven ministates on the Arab side of the Gulf: Abu Dhabi, Dubai, Sharja, Ras al Khaima, Ajman, Umm al-Qaiwain, and Fujaira. Collectively, they share a quarrelsome historical background, and notwithstanding the imbalance caused by Abu Dhabi's wealth, they are at a comparable stage of social development. But Dubai is the natural rival of Abu Dhabi, and Saudi Arabia is fearful of an Abu Dhabi-dominated federation. Thus there are two sets of fears: the smaller states

---

* The Front for the Liberation of Occupied South Yemen.

believe they will one day be "absorbed" by Abu Dhabi, while Abu Dhabi fears that all of the UAE will be annexed by Saudi Arabia.

This fear is a direct consequence of the British evacuation from Aden in 1968 and from the Persian Gulf in December 1971. For until the withdrawals, the deterrent effect of Britain's small ground forces preserved a balance of power in the subregion. Although Iran, Saudi Arabia and Iraq had superior forces, their political effect was not decisive as long as the British military presence remained. Thus in 1961, when the strongest threat to stability came from Iraq and Saudi Arabia, with the former seeking to annex Kuwait and the latter pressing its claims to parts of Qatar and the Trucial States, Britain's willingness to employ force proved sufficient to maintain the status quo. With the British deterrent no longer in the equation, the conflicting ambitions of Saudi Arabia, Iran and Iraq acquire renewed significance.[2]

Throughout the sixties, as Iran became more concerned with militant Arab nationalism to the west and south, it downgraded the traditional Soviet threat from the north. Given Moscow's conciliatory policy toward Iran and Turkey, the Shah argued that the Soviets were less a danger than was the Egyptian military presence in the Arabian Peninsula. His concern over an Egyptian scheme to move through Southern Arabia and capture the oil fields of the peninsula was nevertheless based on the belief that such designs could succeed only with Soviet support. Consequently, the Shah's policy was to woo the Soviets away from strengthening the Egyptian hand. But the same policy meant taking a calculated risk with Moscow and inevitably led the Iranians into a dilemma.

The Soviets, through the Egyptians, not only provided all the military hardware for the Yemen republicans, but also modernized the port of Hodeida and constructed at Sana the longest airstrip—11,500 feet—in the Middle East. The growing Soviet influence in Egypt, Syria and Iraq; their parade of warships in the Mediterranean, the Persian Gulf and the Indian Ocean; their provision of missile-armed boats to Iraq; and their shift to the more radical South Yemen as the focal point of penetration all combined to reinforce the Shah's concern over heightened tensions in the subregion.

It did not escape the Shah that Egypt had the support of both Moscow and Washington. Doubts about American behavior concerning Cyprus, the Kashmir and Yemen led the Shah to believe that in the event of a confrontation with militant Arab nationalism, no aid would be forthcoming from the United States. In addition, the other CENTO allies, Turkey and Pakistan, would themselves be preoccupied with their own regional quarrels. Thus Iranian policy moved perceptibly in the direction of greater independence. Closer relations were forged with the regional opponents of radical Arab nationalism—the Saudis, Yemeni royalists, Jordanians, Kurds and Israelis. In the mid-sixties, Teheran's concern also focused on the Arab threat to Khuzistan, Iran's single most important province because of its strategic position, large oil reserves and important oil installations. In the Arab view, Khuzistan is historically and ethnically Arab. On 11 December 1964, a Conference of Arab Jurists declared the province "an integral part of the Arab homeland," and on 10 November 1965, the Baath regime in Syria did likewise.

Additionally, there were two pressing political and strategic problems. One was the long-standing difference with Iraq regarding navigation rights on the Shatt al-Arab—the river running from the confluence of the Tigris, Euphrates and Karun rivers at the head of the Gulf and forming part of the southern boundary between the two countries. The other was Iran's long-standing claim to Bahrein, which it pressed because of the strategic significance of this small island to the Gulf—from which nearly 86 percent of Middle East petroleum exports and half the world's oil flow. Thus, when the Bahrein issue became entangled with the future of the Trucial States and Qatar, Iran strongly opposed attempts to link Bahrein with the projected Arab federation. At the same time, accommodation with Saudi Arabia led to the establishment in October 1968 of a median line in the Gulf that paved the way for a settlement on Bahrein by the spring of 1970. This accommodation in turn allowed the formation of the United Arab Emirates. Just prior to the UAE's formal creation, Iran asserted its "sovereignty" over the disputed tiny islands of Abu Musa and the two Tumbs. The takeover of the islands in December 1971 and the conciliatory policy in regard to Bahrein were both tied to Teheran's strategic interest in the Strait of Hormuz and the overall security problem of the Gulf. The guiding principles of Iran's security policy gradually emerged as follows: neither superpower should succeed to the former British naval monopoly in the Gulf; Gulf security would be the responsibility of the local powers; Iran should be prepared to act on its own to maintain security in the absence of cooperation at the local level.[3]

Nevertheless, the Shah remained troubled by the danger of Soviet involvement. Soviet influence in Iraq, Afghanistan and India could outflank Iran. A breakup of West Pakistan was regarded as intolerable because of the need to guard the approaches to the Strait of Hormuz and the Gulf. Similarly, it is likely that in the event of a radical coup in any one of the Arab emirates, Iran would intervene militarily across the Gulf as it did with Oman's consent against the Dhofar rebels in 1973. Within two years, the Marxist-led Popular Front for the Liberation of the Occupied Arab Gulf (PFLOAG) was defeated and the rebellion brought to an end.

After the Yom Kippur War, Iran moved toward closer alignment with certain Arab states. Relations with Egypt were reinforced chiefly by means of economic aid. In return, the Shah sought Egyptian noninterference in the affairs of Arabia and the endorsement of Iran's security policy in the Gulf.

More significantly, in March 1975, Iran moved toward accommodation with Iraq and gained recognition of its claim to partial control of the Shatt al-Arab River and rectification of the land borders. In exchange, the Shah agreed to terminate his support to the Kurdish rebels in Iraq by sealing his borders and prohibiting the delivery of any aid.

The American role in the abandonment of the Kurdish struggle is far from obscure and is another example of the defeatist mentality pervading our diplomacy in the region.

As has been clearly established in the now famous secret report of the House Select Subcommittee on Intelligence, chaired by Representative Otis Pike, the Kurds were assured by former President Nixon and Henry Kissinger in June 1972 that the United States would support resumption of their armed rebellion in Iraq.[4] The Kurds, a Muslim but non-Arab people, have risen in revolt against Turkish, British, Persian and Arab rulers throughout the century. Numbering approximately two million, the Iraqi Kurds inhabit a 43,000-square-mile area of mountains, valleys and plains in northern Iraq. Units of Kurdish leader Mulla Mustapha Barzani fought Iraqi forces to a standstill with their guerrilla campaigns from 1961 to 1970, when Baghdad agreed to give them autonomy within four years. The terms of the 11 March 1970 settlement also included Kurdish participation in government, economic development for Kurdish regions and measures recognizing Kurdish cultural and ethnic identity. From the outset it was doubtful the Iraqi government would honor its obligations.

The American decision to support the Kurds was made in response to a specific request by the Shah of Iran, who had earlier pledged assistance to the Kurds in their battle against rival Iraq. Barzani welcomed the American assistance, believing that the American commitment would "guarantee" Iranian support. Interestingly, the timing of the positive American response seems to have been related to Iraq's conclusion of a Treaty of Friendship and Cooperation with the Soviet Union on 9 April 1972, and with the subsequent appointment of two Communists in a cabinet reshuffle and the nationalization of the Iraq Petroleum Company—a consortium of European and American firms. One may speculate which if any of these events prompted the United States commitment to support covertly the Kurdish struggle.

Despite the American pledge, it remains doubtful whether the Nixon-Kissinger intent was to ensure the establishment of an independent sovereign Kurdistan. Such a state might be seen as undermining the security of Iran and Turkey, where sizable Kurdish communities might also seek independence and union with any new state. More likely the American objective was to undermine the Iraqi regime, possibly leading to another coup in Baghdad—whose leaders would allow American companies to operate the rich Kirkuk oil fields. Such American objectives did not, however, conflict with those of the Kurds, who in any case were demanding autonomy, not independence.

The missed opportunity of the Kurds—and the Americans—came during the Yom Kippur War. Iraqi forces were fighting against Israel on the Syrian front and were temporarily distracted from Kurdistan. Israel, anxious to keep the Iraqis engaged at home rather than on the Golan Heights, urged the Kurds to unleash a major offensive. However, in another demonstration of unilateral concession, Kissinger instructed the CIA to advise Barzani not to undertake new offensive operations. This order was all the more astonishing in light of the contrasting Soviet behavior in urging all the Arab states to join the fighting against Israel. Soviet actions in this crisis belied a mutual concern for detente. Nevertheless, Secretary Kissinger seemed determined to make up in American concessions for the Soviet "lapse," and gave more consideration to the military welfare of Iraq—a Soviet ally—than to our natural friends, Israel and the Kurds. The Kissinger "advice" to Barzani was both a disservice to the Kurds and the Israelis and a signal of things to come.

That was October 1973. By April 1975 the Kurdish

resistance suddenly crumbled in the face of a concentrated Iraqi offensive and the termination of American-Iranian aid. This abandonment of the Kurds was preceded by the Iraqi-Iranian border agreement in March 1975.

Two Kurdish scholars argue that Iran reached this agreement with Iraq on instructions from a government in Washington which was anxious to see the matter resolved. "A host of concessions were exacted from Iraq, such as the granting of huge contracts to American corporations to operate in Iraq, the cessation of leftist activities from Iraq against Saudi Arabia, Kuwait, and Iran, and the silencing of Iraqi criticism of Sadat."[5]

Secretary of State Kissinger and other officials deny this accusation, insisting that once Iran and Iraq reached agreement the United States had no alternative but to abandon the Kurds. The Kurds believe otherwise. In their view, it was Washington—not Teheran—that first sold them out.

The fact is that despite the absence of formal diplomatic relations and the vitriolic anti-American rhetoric from Baghdad, American-Iraqi business is increasing dramatically. Recently, the State Department expanded the United States diplomatic "interest section" in Iraq to accommodate this growing trade. Washington has even authorized the sale of the civilian version of the Hercules transport aircraft to Iraq on a commercial basis. This followed a sale in 1975 of eight Boeing jet airliners valued at over $170 million. In addition, American technicians have been brought into Iraq to operate some of its oil fields despite Iraq's nationalization of all its oil resources.

While all this was taking place, the International League for Human Rights, an independent, nongovernmental organization affiliated with the United Nations, charged Iraq on 14 January 1977 with violating the United Nations convention on the elimination of all forms of racial discrimination by systematically attempting "to destroy the political, economic, cultural and linguistic identity of the Kurdish ethnic group."

In a statement sent to the 18 members of the United Nations committee established to monitor the convention, the league presented evidence that Kurdish homes have been confiscated without compensation; that Arab citizens have been settled in those lands; that 30,000 former members of the Kurdish fighting forces have been placed in concentration camps, where they have been beaten and tortured, in contravention of the Iraq amnesty law of 1975; that 227 Kurds have been executed for political reasons; that the Iraqi government has restricted Kurdish ownership of land in oil-rich areas and has authorized the payment of 500 dinars—$1,500—to any Arab who takes a Kurdish spouse.

"The Iraqi government's prewar Arabization policy, that is, the Arabization of Kurdistan and the destruction of Kurdish culture, is still in force," the report said. It added that towns and villages, previously Kurdish, have been resettled with Arabs and renamed with Arab names. It is instructive to note the lack of American concern with these developments when compared to the recurring cries from Washington about Israeli settlement on vacant lands in the West Bank.

The tragic events of the past three years, with Soviet-armed Iraqi forces defeating an American-inspired insurgency, has yet to be fully related. What is now certain is that after encouraging the Kurds to rebel and offering a "guarantee" for continued Iranian support, America, along with Iran, precipitously withdrew its assistance in March 1975, thereby assuring an Iraqi victory. Whether Iran or the United States withdrew first is not the primary issue. The Kurds took to the offensive only because of the American commitment.

Even if it was not Washington that made the first move of betrayal, how does one explain the absence of American pressure on Iran that it not abandon a people who had placed their trust and destiny in an American commitment? Henry Kissinger's statement that "covert action should not be confused with missionary work" is, unwittingly, a lesson for all oppressed freedom-loving peoples not to confuse their aspirations for human rights with American so-called interests and "guarantees." The Kurds were done in not by their enemies but by their friends.[6]

It is little wonder that matters evolved as tragically as they did in the Kurdish affair given the predominance of defeatism in American foreign policy circles. American dishonor in this affair is one more example of the bitter fruits we continue to harvest from our politics of defeat. Most ironic of all, our ally Iran has also learned something about American weakness from the deferential way in which we, in the best of interpretations, allowed them to abandon the Kurds.

It can be little expected that Iran will continue to bear the burden and risks of defending pro-Western interests in the region when American policy in this regard is both fretful and indecisive. The Shah of Iran prides himself on being a good judge of character, both national and personal. He worries about our reliability in the defense of Western security in the Middle East. He is not alone in this concern, for Turkey among other powers also has its doubts about America's inertia in the face of a growing Soviet challenge.

An illuminating sequel to the Iranian-Iraqi "settlement" of 1975 is Iraq's renewed demands for Warba and Bubiyan, two islands near the mouth of the Shatt al-Arab River, which are part of Kuwait. The Iraqis claim both and want to build a new deep water port on Bubiyan—to be open, of course, to Soviet warships. This issue first surfaced in March 1973, when Iraqi troops attacked two Kuwaiti border outposts and took up positions on Kuwaiti territory before subsequently withdrawing. Again in 1976, after an Iraqi force crossed the desert border and took up positions inside Kuwait, the latter openly demanded that Iraq withdraw its troops. Relations between these two Arab states remain strained and must be viewed in the context of Iraq's dormant claim to all of Kuwait. In 1961, it was Britain's military deployment that had deterred an Iraqi threat to invade and annex Kuwait. Today, it is Iran that expresses concern about preserving Kuwait's integrity against Iraqi claims. One would have thought that the American-Iranian offering up of their Kurdish prize would have moderated Iraqi actions. It hasn't, principally because of the abiding Soviet designs for the region.

The Soviets recognize the subregion for what it truly is: an area of inter-Arab and Arab-Iranian rivalries that can be fully exploited by Moscow at the opportune time in its global strategy. When the Kremlin is ready, it will pass the word to Iraq that her "manifest destiny" southward into Arabia can finally be realized through Soviet neutralization of Iran and with the cooperation of a defeatist United States. To be sure, there will always be a few "realists" who will contend that an Iraqi takeover of Arabia might "stabilize" the area.

VIII

ARAB OIL AND
THREATS TO
WESTERN
SECURITY

S UPPORT for the Arab case against Israel in the
United States is advanced primarily by those with
business and commercial interests in the region. First, the
Arabs are far more numerous and widely distributed
throughout the region possessing both territory and resources, chiefly oil and, more recently, money. In view
of the growing dependence of the United States on Middle East oil and that of our European allies and Japan
for the bulk of their oil supplies, it is clear that the
industrial democracies have a vital interest in retaining
access to Arab oil. Moreover, the oil-producing countries
are acquiring a growing financial capacity to influence
both foreign policies of other governments and the international monetary system.

Consequently, given the fact that two-thirds of the free world's crude oil reserves are in the region, that American dependency may grow even greater over the next decade, that economic health and perhaps political survival in Western Europe and Japan depend on the continued flow of Middle East oil and that Arabs are willing and able to use oil exports as a political weapon, it is conveniently argued that it is necessary in the national interest to withdraw support from Israel in order to assure access to that indispensable commodity. After first looking at the role of oil politics itself, we shall have a better grasp of the spurious nature of this argument.

In any discussion of the Middle East, the energy crisis and the complex role of oil must be understood. It is estimated that the world as a whole will use as much energy in the 30-year period 1970 to the year 2000 as it did from the start of mankind to 1970. It is this massive growth in the use of fossil fuels which mainly created the energy crisis now confronting the United States and many countries of the world.

At the heart of the problem is the growing consumption of oil by Western Europe, Japan and the United States. The world uses about 51 million barrels of oil per day (mb/d) of which the United States, with only 4½% of the population, uses one-third. International oil companies, faced with demands of host countries for more revenue at a time when oil import restrictions were in effect at home while special tax incentives existed for producing oil abroad, proceeded during the 1950s to convert Western Europe and Japan from coal to oil.[1] Thus, we are no longer the only large market for oil but must compete with our allies for supplies. The resulting vulnerability of the West provides a tempting target for the Arabs and the Soviet Union for future mischief. American oil companies have played a vital role in the deepening crisis of the United States. As revealed in hearings before the 1974 Senate Subcommittee on Multinational Corporations, the international oil companies were given secret tax considerations in 1950 for overseas oil operations.[2] Later, in 1953, the oil companies were given principal responsibility for molding American foreign policy in the Middle East as recommended in a then secret memorandum to the National Security Council signed by the secretaries of state, defense and interior.[3] Much of the pro-Arab bias of the United States during the Sinai Campaign of 1956 and the failure to find a permanent peace in the Middle East can be traced to these secret actions which were never debated or approved by Congress or known to the American people. Indeed, as shown by such actions during and since the Yom Kippur War, Senators Frank Church and Henry Jackson have pointed out that the international oil companies, far from being agents of the United States as expected in a time of crisis, were in fact agents of the Arab governments acting against the common strategic interests of the United States and Israel. The very term "multinational corporation" has become a cover for giant, basically American companies operating on the world scene and even at home in direct opposition to American national security interests when such interests do not coincide with their own broad pecuniary gain. As a matter of record in Congressional testimony, these multinational oil corporations were the executors of the direct orders of the Saudi Government for the Oil Embargo of 1973–74 against the industrial democracies thus undermining the United States strategic interest in the economic vitality of the Western Alliance. Even shipments to the United States Navy were not excluded from this embargo.

The Arabs now dominate for political purposes an astonishingly powerful international oil cartel, the Organization of Petroleum Exporting Countries (OPEC), which consists not of corporations, but of sovereign nations backed by diplomatic, economic and military power. Mistakes in United States policy have been of great assistance to the success of OPEC. It must be remembered that the United States Government advised the oil companies and foreign governments not to resist OPEC at the critical Teheran Conference in 1971 at which the fateful decisions to embark on a series of oil price rises were taken.[4] James E. Akins was director of the State Department's Office of Fuels and Energy at the time and was later fired as ambassador to Saudi Arabia reportedly for being too pro-Saudi. Henry M. Schuler, vice-president of Hunt International Petroleum Corp., third largest in Libya, told the Church Subcommittee in 1974 that "if a political and economic monster has been loosed upon the world, it is the creation of western governments and oil companies. Together, we created it and gave it the necessary push; so only we, acting in harmony, can slow it down." Pierre Rinfret, a respected international economic advisor, informs us that humanity faces a worldwide depression because the oil-rich Arab countries are determined to destroy Israel and will bleed the energy-starved Western world unless better leadership is shown.[5] Factors in OPEC's strength are oil company collaboration, failure of Western reaction and Soviet backing and abetment.

The *Congressional Quarterly* of October 1975 concluded that "the United States faces, any time that OPEC is emboldened to hike its prices, such results as a further drain on consumer purchasing power, another spur to inflation, deeper deficits in our balance of payments and the federal budget and an ever increasing menace to the world economic system."

It is clear that OPEC has been able to frustrate the two major goals of the energy policy of the United States, namely: to lower unreasonable international oil prices and to reduce dependence on unreliable foreign sources. With respect to prices, OPEC has been able to increase them 10% in October 1975 and 5–10% in January 1977 on top of the devastating 400% boosts in 1973 despite worldwide recession and huge shutdown in production capacity varying from 6 to 13 mb/d. During 1974, the International Monetary Fund reported that OPEC countries received a fantastic oil income of $133 billion. This income resulted in an OPEC trade surplus of $97 billion and a world deficit of an equal amount. OPEC received comparable income in 1975 and 1976. Investment income alone for 1975 of $7 billion, according to oil consultant Walter Levy, exceeded OPEC's entire oil income in 1970. Less Developed Countries (LDC) owe the industrial West more than $170 billion, principally for oil purchases during the last three years with repayment uncertain. The world has lost about $600 billion in GNP during this period, spreading misery and political instability everywhere. In the United States, the unwarranted oil price increases will result in 1977 in the loss of $75 billion in GNP, $90 billion in disposable income and 3 million jobs.[6] This is a terrible price to pay for an inept foreign policy which refuses to see the disastrous social and political consequences of appeasing OPEC. It is the vast sums of money flowing to OPEC that is the short-sighted reason for much of the support of American businessmen for Arab political goals. During 1976, the United States paid $36 billion for imported oil. This sum is more, in constant dollars, than the entire Marshall Plan cost of rebuilding Western Europe after WW II. Recalling that a trade deficit of only $6.4 billion in 1972 forced the United States into two currency devaluations and other hardships, it is not too difficult to realize the massive unemployment and inflation that have been generated throughout the world as the effects both of shifting real wealth to OPEC and of high energy costs trickled through world economies. Clearly, the primary goal of the United States to reduce international oil prices has failed thus far. The challenge is to employ our national strengths in trade, technology and food in a more effective manner to accomplish this objective.

The second national goal to increase domestic energy supplies continued to falter during 1976. Project Independence has been virtually abandoned, imports have increased and domestic production is falling—still disadvantaged by lack of the kinds of United States tax incentives enjoyed by OPEC oil. A key factor is that under present policies and tax laws, it is more profitable to import Arab oil than to develop domestic energy sources. During 1976, imports exceeded 7.0 mb/d compared to 6.1 million in 1973. Development of environmentally acceptable coal, nuclear energy, shale and offshore oil is far behind schedule. Our Canadian neighbor was the largest supplier of oil to the United States in

1973–74. Nigeria supplanted Canada in 1975 as our largest supplier of imported oil and was in turn replaced by Saudi Arabia in 1976. In 1974, Saudi Arabia supplied the United States with only 2.4% of its oil or 433,000 bpd; 544,000 bpd in 1975 and 1,063,000 bpd in 1976. It is not clear whether the recent large increase in United States imports of Saudi oil was due to necessity or to other factors such as private arrangements between Saudi Arabia and Aramco. Downstream use by the United States of refineries and shipping recently acquired by the Saudis is increasing rapidly. Such use further enhances the vulnerability of the United States to a future Saudi embargo.

Any future oil embargo is likely to be guided by the principles laid down by Dr. Mustafa Khalil in his study of the oil weapon for *Al Ahram*'s Institute for Strategic Studies and used by President Sadat and Saudi Arabia during the 1973–74 embargo.[7] These can be paraphrased as follows: oil is a strategic and economic weapon, not a weapon of war; it can therefore be best used politically to achieve Arab aims; oil can guarantee access to arms; it can be used to provoke European and Japanese pressure on the United States in furtherance of Arab goals; in this strategy it is necessary to avoid making enemies of the consuming countries; above all, unity of action among the United States, Western Europe and Japan must be prevented by proffering "guarantees" of a continuous flow of oil to Western Europe and Japan.

It is time for the United States to recognize that employment of the oil weapon during a time of peace to achieve strategic aims is a form of hostile petrowarfare that is crippling the West and paving the way for Soviet subversion of the weakened countries allied to the United

States.[8] Israel has withstood alone for many years a total Arab oil embargo. Western Europe and Japan are now threatened. It is time to face up to the world challenge of an Arab-dominated oil cartel which is more dependent on the United States than the reverse. The United States can, if it will, grant or withhold bilateral trade in items needed by the Arab oil powers in order to assure access to oil imports at reasonable prices. It is clear as a starter that negotiations with OPEC should be removed from the oil companies and centralized in high government office with authority to bring the full strength of the United States to bear on all aspects of this challenge. It is time to remove special incentives for current OPEC oil producers and give them to domestic oil.[9]

The financial and political erosion of the Western world can be stopped by sound policies favoring our allies and friends, not our oil adversaries. To ignore the challenge of OPEC is to accept the gradual loss of independence and well-being. It is time for the American body politic to affirm once and for all that our government at least was not created to foster the further enrichment of the very few. Present OPEC oil policy and our politics of defeat in not confronting it will otherwise sap not so much the arteries of our industry as the blood vessels of our national body and our moral tissue.

Let us now look at the argument that access to oil can be assured by disengaging from our commitments to Israel. Setting aside for the moment all other considerations, even an American abandonment of Israel would still not provide insurance against a renewed Arab embargo. Pursuant to an Arab summit conference in Algiers in November 1973, the white regimes of South Africa and Rhodesia were subject to a total embargo along with Portugal. While the latter had allowed United States aircraft to refuel at the Azores on their way to Israel during the October 1973 airlift, neither South Africa nor Rhodesia had anything to do with the Arab-Israeli conflict. The embargo was meant to be a visible expression of Arab solidarity with Black Africa. The fact that a disguised form of black slavery is still prevalent in much of Arabia does not inhibit the Arabs from cashing in on the political capital of oil against the racist regimes of southern Africa. Thus readiness to impose an oil embargo for political reasons unrelated to the Arab-Israeli conflict cannot be dismissed. Even if the United States were to abandon Israel altogether, the reimposition of an embargo is possible as retaliation for any American action meant to bring down the price of oil or any legislation restricting Arab petrodollar investments in the United States.[10] In fact, the absence of a vibrant Israeli presence would encourage such acts by simply making them safer.

While the United States will remain dependent on oil imports for at least a decade, not all foreign producers are alike. Unlike the Arab producers, none of the non-Arab oil producers has used oil as a political weapon. Therefore, to the extent possible, the national interest would best be served by a policy of preferring non-Arab producers. The possibility of the United States choosing a discriminatory international energy policy complemented and enhanced by a major effort to increase domestic production is not only desirable but feasible.[11] It would furthermore be possible to limit current oil investment incentives abroad only to present nonproducers and impoverished developing countries in a new dynamic program of international "affirmative action."

The United States does not have to be independent of foreign oil in order to be impervious to political demands from the Arab oil producing states. A meaningful energy policy encompassing broad conservation and development of both hydrocarbons and new energy sources would assure the United States an ability to withstand blackmail.[12] Active involvement by the American people in the achievement of energy goals would be one of the principal benefits of a manifestation of United States leadership in this regard. With this personal involvement, Americans would be far less willing to bend to extortionist demands. Blackmail without the victim's fear cannot succeed.

All this is not to say that the United States may be indifferent to the availability of Arab oil. Aside from a more marginal American demand for Arab oil, Western Europe and Japan are heavily dependent on it for most of their energy needs and will remain so for the foreseeable future. It is apparent that for the West the security of the oil deposits is assured to a much greater extent under a conservative monarch than a radical leader. Thus, to the extent that the existence and vitality of Israel diverts the attentions and energies of the Arab radicals, the conservative oil producers are net beneficiaries. Moreover, in the event of a consumer-producer confrontation forced on the West as a result of high oil prices, the presence in the Middle East of a powerful Israel would prove to be of great value.

Under the impact of the Arab oil weapon, the unity of Europe is now in jeopardy and the very fabric of

European society seriously threatened. By alternately quadrupling its prices and cutting off oil, the Arab world brought an abrupt end to the European prosperity which developed since 1948 behind the American shield. The Soviet role and American acquiescence in this affair must be accorded full recognition. The record shows that Moscow urged use of the oil weapon against the West long before the Arabs had agreed among themselves to do so. Soviet broadcasts in Arabic as well as press and periodical commentaries have publicized Western dependence and therefore vulnerability to oil pressure. Not only did Moscow promise instant success but also instructed the Arabs in the most effective ways of employing the weapon.[13]

By revealing the weakness of European unity, by fostering economic rivalries and suspicions within the European Economic Community, by inciting Arabs to play the oil consumers against each other and by provoking serious discord within the Atlantic alliance, Moscow has encouraged a process favoring revolutionary disruption of the Western alliance network. In effect, the free world strategy of containing Communist influence is failing rapidly. European unity has been shaken, energy prices have skyrocketed, thus threatening European economic stability and Third World development prospects. The developing countries now demand a fundamental revision of the world economic order, and Moscow is better able to exploit rivalries within the Western camp.

Concurrently, the OPEC cartel exercises an inordinate influence on the West's way of life, fanning inflation and plunging most countries into depression at home and deficits in their balance of payments abroad. Unimpressed with arguments that economic misery in the West—and outright famine in the poorer countries—would damage their interests too, the oil cartel believes it has the world by the neck. They seem determined to squeeze hard enough to rule out real economic health but not quite enough to strangulate. Great nations bow gratefully to only "incremental" price increases while poorer countries hold out their begging bowls—avoiding the faintest whisper of reproach against the oil producers. And yet, the cumulative impact of the wrecking process continues: a matter of slow but steady battering of the fragile process of economic recovery. Observers now question whether the existing political and social structure in the industrial democracies can survive protracted economic stagnation and decline. But for the Arab conviction that fear of Soviet interposition nullifies the Western military option to seize the oil fields, would the oil cartel risk economic warfare with Western industrial society? This conviction is basically unfounded since a forthright and determined American policy will not be challenged militarily by the Soviet Union. The Kremlin has no national interest at stake in the affair, being basically self-sufficient in oil.

The oil-rich states of Arabia—Saudi Arabia, Kuwait, and Abu Dhabi—while the wealthiest, are the most vulnerable links in the OPEC chain of strangulation. These states are sparsely populated and receive oil revenues way beyond their most extravagant needs. Saudi Arabia, with a population of 5 million, has an annual oil income of $27 billion. Kuwait, with a meager population of 900,-000, only half of whom are nationals, receives oil revenues of $8 billion. Finally, Abu Dhabi, with a nomadic population of only 50,000, has annual revenues in excess of $5 billion.

By contrast, Iran with $19 billion in annual revenues has to feed a rapidly expanding population now already at 35 million people. Iraq, a covetous Arab state of the region, has to support a population of 11 million and can barely make ends meet with oil revenues of $7 billion.

It is therefore incumbent upon American foreign policy-makers to stress that but for United States sufferance and implicit military guarantee, the autocratic rulers of the independent oil states of Arabia would be swept away. As a result, we should expect the proper degree of concern for our own national interests when the subject of oil prices is on the table—not the degree of their further increase, but rather the magnitude of their reduction. In order to maintain the natural laws of supply and demand, such reductions in price would be brought about through sharp increases in production in conjunction with an appropriate 30-year pricing policy, guaranteeing the solvency of producer and consumer at each end of that time span. To accomplish this objective, however, we must effectively remove the multinational oil companies from their role of "honest broker" in support of Arab oil interests and their own private gain.

Some may raise objections to the implementation of such a concerted strategy to stop the incessant undermining of the industrial democracies and the poor developing countries. Some may point to the oil spigot and cry "embargo." The answer is a simple one. With a policy of pressure against the weakest links of OPEC, the oil-rich states of Arabia will quickly learn to live with the realities of Western power in the region, especially when it continues to pay reasonably well. In the final analysis they will not trade in their Mercedes and Cadillacs for a Russian Troika. Only by economic alliance with the West can the oil-rich states continue to establish the kind of economic security for themselves that they will require toward the end of the century when the price of oil starts to collapse. The Arabs realize that when it becomes more profitable to invest oil wealth in the bank rather than in the ground, they will find no suitable banks for such a purpose in the Soviet bloc.

IX

THE PROBLEM
OF PALESTINE

A major misconception guiding American politics of
defeat in the region is the assumption that the central
issue in the Arab-Israeli conflict is the "Palestinian problem." There is an issue with regard to Palestine, but it
is not that of the Arab Palestinians. It is rather that
Palestine is a country in dispute between two nationalisms,
only one of which is prepared to compromise.

Hebrew nationalism is coalescing successfully in that
part of historic Palestine which is today the democratic
state of Israel. On the other hand, the Arabs of Palestine,
mostly citizens of the Hashemite Kingdom of Jordan,
demand a second Arab state, in fact a third state in
historic mandated Palestine. They are in dispute among
themselves over their own national identity, whether it

is Jordanian, Palestinian or simply Arab. However, they are certain in their resolve to uproot Jewish nationalism from the region.

The danger inherent in the creation of a third Palestinian state in the region can be seen from a sober analysis of the Arab-Israeli conflict. The heart of that conflict is not the aggrieved Arab people of Palestine, loosely called Palestinians, but the unwillingness of the Arabs to accept the reality of a sovereign Israeli nation and state in the Middle East. The historic fact that the Jews were the only people to have established and developed an indigenous independent cultural and national existence in what is historic Palestine is not permitted to confuse the Arabs in their dream of renewed Arab and Islamic dominance of the Middle East. Drawing on a fundamental sectarian outlook on the world, the Arabs, until now frustrated by repeated military defeats, have vastly raised their expectations because of new oil wealth. The fact that some Arabs may have suffered during the period of the reestablishment of Jewish sovereignty over a part of Palestine is the direct result of a stubborn refusal to reconcile themselves to its existence. It is not avowed grievances which keep them from accepting Israel, but rather the claim of the Jews to a state of their own in the region. The fact that the majority of Israelis are refugees from Arab lands where they were a barely tolerated and despised minority only adds to the "effrontery."

Concessions by Israel which weaken the state militarily and morally and place her in a position of greater dependence for her security on external guarantees would only increase Arab determination to exorcise the Jewish state from their midst. It follows, therefore, that the only way the Arab leaders and masses can ever be brought to an even begrudging acceptance of Israel is to maintain Israel's deterrent capacity at a high level. Proposals for a new Arab state in central Palestine work in exactly the opposite sense.

Until the Yom Kippur War, the "Palestinian issue" did not play a central role in the conflict. In the post-1973 period, however, it was being increasingly pushed to the fore by Arab governments. There was also a distinct overlap of Arab and Soviet interests on this score. Moscow moved gradually toward a position of outright support of the so-called Palestine Liberation Organization (PLO), at times even voicing criticism of Arab—especially Egyptian—lack of sufficient support for the organization.

The Palestinian issue can be better understood in the context of the entire range of interests involved. Instead of engaging in such a probing analysis, American decision-makers content themselves with accepting the Arab insistence on the vital importance of the issue at its face value. The PLO, it should be remembered, was a creation of Nasser's first Arab summit meeting in 1964. It was meant to serve as an Egyptian tool in the effort to regain Egyptian leadership of the Arab world and a convenient weapon against Israel. The Arab defeat in 1967 and the subsequent rise of Al-Fatah as an independent military arm of the PLO reduced its role as a puppet of the Egyptians. Although Egypt and most Arab governments were wary of the PLO's radicalism and growing independence, they nevertheless espoused its goals to the full and incorporated them with their own in a phased plan of action.

There exists an apparent contradiction between the all-out Arab support of the PLO and its goals and the conduct of individual Arab governments toward the organization. The dividing line is that which pertains to the safety and internal stability of individual Arab regimes. There never was any disagreement between Arab leaders on the importance of the PLO (or its predecessors) as a major weapon directed against Israel. Not one Arab government has ever disassociated itself from the PLO National Covenant of 1968 which formally denies the legitimacy of the Jewish state, calls for its elimination and for the expulsion of the majority of its Jewish citizens.[1] All Arab governments, in varying degrees, support the most extreme terrorist outrages against Israel and willingly grant asylum to the perpetrators. This attitude of support would change very radically, however, whenever an Arab government felt that the Palestinians were being used by another Arab government as a tool against them or when the PLO itself acted in any way that threatened the stability or safety of an Arab regime. In such cases, treatment of Palestinians was ruthless. They were butchered mercilessly by the Jordanian army in September 1970, by the Lebanese and Syrian armies in 1975–1976, and individual members of various Palestinian organizations were sometimes summarily publicly executed in Iraq, Jordan and Syria.

No less vicious is the fratricidal warfare between various Palestinian factions, especially between those supported by different Arab governments that are antagonistic to one another. The net result so far has been that Palestinian Arabs have sustained more human loss from

Arab armies and from each other than they did at the hands of Israel's military.

The commitment of Arab governments and society in general to the PLO and its goals should not be under-estimated, in spite of the severe punishment inflicted on it by these same governments. Arab unity and the dream of a united Arab superpower—a kind of modern caliphate —is very real in Arab literature, speeches and political platforms. It is further from realization today than it was thirty-two years ago when the Arab League was established with seven member states. Absence of prog-ress toward unity, coupled with the periodic rise and fall of so many short-lived paper unions and federations, has led to frustration. This was compounded by the failure of the Arabs to prevent the establishment in their midst of what they consider to be an alien entity and the periodic military defeats they sustained at its hands.

Over the years, all such pent-up frustrations have been directed by Arab leaders against Israel. This struggle has served as a convenient excuse for lack of progress, both in terms of domestic development and in the quest for Arab unity. The only unity that was ever achieved in those decades was during the peak moments of con-frontation with Israel. Between these moments the conflict served as a whip and a slogan to be used against enemies, whether domestic, inter-Arab or international. In inter-Arab parlance, the gravest charge and the greatest insult was that of a sellout to Israel.[2]

On this background, the PLO or the Palestinians came to fulfill an important and useful role, politically and psychologically. It became the repository of the Arab cause against Israel, the standard bearer that was capable of delivering blows against the enemy when the Arab states were too weak or incapable of acting for fear of reprisal. It also provided a convenient cover behind which the Arab governments could better prepare themselves for outright military action. The Palestinians, as individuals, are by and large despised and even persecuted in the Arab countries, but the PLO as a movement, as an idea, is universally supported and even idealized throughout the Arab states.

The transient identity of interests between the PLO and the Arab governments has been given clear expression on the strategic level as well. This has often been reiterated by Arab leaders, even as they clashed with Palestinian organizations on the tactical level. Over the recent years, this strategy developed into something that can be likened to a phased plan that is designed to serve the needs of all the interested Arab states. It lends itself to moderate and extreme interpretation at one and the same time. Roughly, it combines the elements of *time*— a stage-by-stage advance toward the final goal—and *space* —a gradual constriction of Israel geographically and politically until it is reduced to a state of submission.

In essence, the strategy is a natural outcome of the series of military defeats sustained by the Arab states since 1949. The previously openly declared goal of solving the conflict by military means was set aside because it served only to strengthen American support for Israel. The task has now been entrusted to the Palestinians whose lack of governmental status enables them to continue fighting in a "war of liberation." The Arab governments, and especially Egypt, set their sights on more realistic, attainable short-range objectives. Thus, the Yom Kippur

War was the first Arab war with limited military objectives combined with specific political goals. The exercise was aimed primarily at the United States, with the intention of driving the first wedge between it and Israel.

Obviously, the readjustment of strategy was not easily achievable in the Arab context. Those who focused on short-term goals opened themselves to attack by other Arab governments and, of course, by the Palestinians. Nevertheless, Sadat was able to mobilize sufficient support for his phased plan of action. Another potent source of support was Henry Kissinger. He had realized very early in his involvement in the Middle East that as long as the Arabs focused on long-range goals in the conflict, the United States would have to remain solidly behind Israel. As soon as Sadat seemed to give up Nasser's previous objectives and spoke of peace in the Middle East, even if only for "the next generation," the United States could step in and play a role that assured it a position of influence in both camps. Sadat could now show his critics that he was capable of weaning the United States away from Israel, of regaining territories from Israel without losing sight of or commitment to the Arab strategic goal in the conflict with Israel. It is here that the PLO plays a crucial role.

The Arab demands of Israel have undergone a process of redefinition in accordance with the "phased" plan. The negative resolution of the September 1967 Khartoum Arab Summit meeting—no peace (with Israel), no recognition and no negotiations—was set aside. A different two-tier approach was adopted: withdrawal of Israel from territories occupied in June 1967 and return of the "rights" of the Palestinians. The first is a concrete, unequivocal demand. The second part is deliberately left unclear: it is either left to the PLO to define what would constitute a regaining of Palestinian rights, or else reference is made to the need to establish a Palestinian "national entity" in those territories west of the Jordan River that were in Arab hands before June 1967. The term "national entity" had been chosen so as to distinguish it from a "state," because the only state the PLO would be willing to accept in the context of a final settlement is that which stretches throughout mandated Palestine, encompassing what are now Israel and Jordan.

The phased plan enabled Sadat of Egypt and Assad of Syria to disengage somewhat from Palestinian goals and adopt an image of moderation and willingness to forsake extreme and hitherto unattainable objectives that had cast them in a negative light. An added advantage was the positive popular reaction in some of the Arab states to a new trend of passing the onus of achieving Palestinian goals to the Palestinians themselves. Finally, under the "phased" heading, Arab confrontation states were permitted to conclude interim or temporary agreements with Israel in return for Israeli withdrawal from territory, providing they did not prejudice future Arab demands on Israel.

In the strategic military sphere, the Arab governments, led by Egypt's Sadat, are applying the lessons of the wars of 1967 and 1973. In the Six Day War they failed to take full advantage of the geographic layout that would have enabled the Arab armies to cut Israel into four or five pieces by one determined, coordinated surprise assault. Israel took the initiative and carried the battle into enemy territory from the very beginning.

In the Yom Kippur War, the Egyptian and Syrian armies did mount a surprise, massive and coordinated invasion. This time, however, it was Israel's territorial depth that saved the day. The meager units on the front lines fought a delaying action while giving some ground until reinforcements arrived. Had the same battle been waged on the 1967 lines, Israel may well have found itself cut into pieces. The Arab phased plan for the solution of the Jewish question in the Middle East is simply to reestablish the conditions that would strategically reduce Israel to submission.

Since the immediate Arab objective is the return to the 1967 lines, conflicts of interest that may arise in the course of the implementation of their plan are brushed aside.

In sum, if the Arab phased plan were to be seen for what it is, and the PLO denied the role of serving as a front for the achievement of that plan, the real dimensions of a Hashemite-Palestinian contest for power would emerge. Ever since King Abdullah annexed the West Bank to his kingdom in 1950, a clash has existed between the Palestinian Arab elite and the Hashemite ruling family. In spite of its revolutionary, pan-Arab and anti-Israel ideologies, the PLO is engaged in the same power contest over the control of that part of Palestine which was renamed Jordan in 1950.

Willingly or not the establishment of a third state in Palestine between Israel and the Hashemite kingdom of Jordan would undermine Israel's security in fact as well as in the minds of the region's peoples. A compromise reached within the context of a peace treaty between Israel and its Jordanian Palestinian neighbors to the east is the only remedy. It would not only infer, but actually promote, a new sense of living together in a framework of shared responsibilities and mutual acceptance.

Serious recommendations for an independent "Palestinian state" alongside Israel and Jordan, with or without the Palestinian Liberation Organization (PLO), would constitute a grave threat to both Israel and Jordan. In terms of tranquility for the region's peoples, it is irrelevant whether representatives of the PLO or any of its constituent affiliates take over, join with, or are totally excluded from the government of such a rump state.

America's interests in the region are peace, stability, access to oil and a strong Israel capable of acting effectively as a strategic asset in the expanse of water and land between the Mediterranean Sea and the Persian Gulf.

The Soviet Union's imperial interests in the region do not initially relate to any overt takeover, but rather to the fomenting of instability in the Middle East which can be exploited to deny the West and Japan the sustenance of Arab oil and the full benefit of the Israeli asset.

It is a sign of America's decline in the Middle East and our international politics of defeat that policymakers would create in a new Palestinian state the very conditions for our final demise as a power of consequence in the region. Studiously ignored is the estimate that the Soviet empire does not have to take over a single oil well or a hectare of desert to accomplish this feat. They have a pliant surrogate in the Arabs. Some American pundits in a moment of misconception have proposed that a viable solution for peace in the Middle East must incorporate the Soviet Union as a party. In reality this approach is the sure way to guarantee failure so long as the Soviet Union retains its continuing imperial dreams against the liberal democracies. The one Arab state that America might have relied upon, Lebanon, has been effectively crippled and is now subject to Syrian domination in the true sense of a protectorate. For American policymakers to hint at the creation of a third Palestinian state and an accommodation with the PLO is to play directly into Soviet hands. Let us look at the specific reasons on the terrain why the proposal for a third Palestinian state is untenable if American security interests and assets in the region are to be maintained.

A third Palestinian state would insert a new element of instability in the region as a vehicle for Soviet machinations. By definition, a third Palestinian state would not be subject to internal control by either Israel or Jordan. Consequently, the United States and Israel would be asked to rely on the Arabs themselves to suppress terrorism and on the Soviet Union to discourage it. In reality, the opposite would be the case. Free of effective Israeli or Jordanian control, the area would evolve into a hotbed of irredentism and terror, starting first among the local Arab inhabitants. At the same time, this terrorism would spill into Israel and Jordan. No Palestinian government would be able to control terrorism even should it wish to do so, no more than the Irish Republic and the United Kingdom can suppress the terror and armed incursions of the Provisional IRA in Ulster.

The Soviet grand design for exploiting a new Arab state in Palestine is being actively sketched at the present time. The Kremlin's intention is to establish such a state as a kind of Cuba for the Middle East. One might concede that such a state would not or could not be used by the Arabs as a springboard against Israel. However, it would most assuredly be used by the Soviets as a launching pad against Jordan, Saudi Arabia and the oil emirates. The opening for direct Soviet military presence in the Middle East would finally have become a reality through Palestine.

There should be no doubt that Moscow would actively promote the conversion of any new Palestinian state into a solid base from which to promote subversion and revolution throughout the region.[3] This could be so orchestrated as to provoke a military and revolutionary crisis in the Middle East from such a nerve center all the way to the Persian Gulf. This could be done when the Soviets would have tactical and strategic need of diverting the attention of Israel—and of America—from their movements elsewhere. The added conspiracy with radical elements to destroy the oil fields and pipelines of Arabia would further undercut the security, fighting ability and will of the West. Should the current United States politics of defeat continue, Moscow would rely on Washington as in the past to deter Israel from any "precipitous" action against "minor" terrorist infractions until the Soviets themselves, and only they, would have need of a conflagration. As always, NATO, not the Middle East, would be the Soviet objective. In sum, any truncated new Arab state established in Palestine would serve as a Soviet *agent provocateur*.

At the same time as Moscow would be fomenting radical operations through the proposed state, Russia would also develop its conventional military infrastructure. Such an infrastructure could accommodate the Arabs or a direct Soviet intervention at a time of their own choosing.

Today, the Soviets have to consider the sobering disadvantages of direct intervention on the Arab side from the geographic periphery of the conflict. With a new Arab state established in Palestine and Israel's defense perimeter accordingly narrowed, Moscow would have the geographic advantage of being able to intervene militarily in the very heart of the conflict. The Soviets would calculate that they could do so before Israel could adequately react. Russia would thus be in a position to neutralize the only sure asset America has in the region. It is erroneous to delude ourselves that Moscow needs to maintain Israel as a reason for the Arabs to seek Soviet support and involvement in the region. Rather, the dismemberment of Israel would leave the Arab world free to explode in social revolution as feudal and radical groups and societies discovered each other rather than Israel as their greatest enemy. In this context, the Soviet Union would be able to squeeze the monarchy of Jordan between a radicalized Palestinian state and an aggressive Syria still dreaming of pan-Arab glory.

It has been contended that the conservative monarchies of Jordan and Saudi Arabia would not permit what otherwise would be a natural process of radicalization in the proposed state. This projection is untenable when viewed in the context of intra-Arab fratricidal strife and Soviet designs for the region. At the same time, one would hope that those proposing Saudi or Hashemite control of the situation in central Palestine do not envisage the stationing of Arab "peacekeeping" forces in that region.

Once a base for armed underground mobilization had been established in Palestine, the situation would become intolerable. There would always be a rejectionist PLO that would continue the cause of Israel's destruction however much the government of a Palestinian state would wish to mobilize its resources for conventional confrontation. The struggle would continue between radical leaders who abjure even a temporary compromise with Israel and the "moderates" seeking the development of another confrontation state, this time in the very heart of Palestine.

Should a new Arab state in Palestine become an advance base for antiaircraft missiles and long-range artillery, it would serve a critical military role in the next confrontation with Israel. It does no good for American commentators to remark that Israel would be more of a military threat to such a state than vice versa. Such an argument overlooks the presence of the surrounding Arab armies in Egypt, Syria and Jordan, ready to exploit the Palestinian Arabs militarily at the opportune moment. In fact, recent tragic events prove that the Syrian leaders and Hashemite rulers would be prepared to fight ignobly to the last Palestinian. They would know better than any American armchair strategist that the Arab East can survive the devastation of the Arab-inhabited towns of Palestine, but Israel cannot long survive with its cities, highways and airways converted into battlefields.

So long as Israel were in a position of insecurity, threatened constantly with the erosion of its morale and dependent on external guarantees, the end objective would remain: to move Israel from the borders of 1967 to the crazy-quilt lines of 1947 and finally to the waters of the Mediterranean where American ships skilled in evacuation procedures would perhaps be allowed to pick up the survivors in one act of Soviet-Arab magnanimity.

The proposed Palestinian entity would become the

sanctuary for irredentism and terror. Cut off from independent access to the sea, confined to the rocky highlands of Judea and Samaria, its people would never be satisfied with their place in the region. Even though a substantial part of the middle class might perhaps acquiesce in this state of affairs, the illusion of independence would only encourage its effective exercise against the encircling power, Israel. The fact that such a rump state would at the same time surround Jewish Jerusalem and stretch to within 9 miles of the Mediterranean at Israel's narrowest point is sure to encourage a radical minority to oppose by force of arms the unavoidable limits placed on such a state.

Manifestly, the proposed rump state would not be economically viable. This condition would only be aggravated by the opening of its borders to the one million oppressed Palestinians living in the neighboring Arab states. Whatever economic chance there might be for a rump state in the Judean and Samarian hills would be immediately negated by any sizable influx. The deteriorating economic condition would exacerbate the political climate in the territory. One might argue that the Arab inhabitants of the West Bank after ten years of beneficial exposure are somehow prepared to make their peace with the Israelis. The exact opposite need be said for those Palestinian Arabs who continue to survive in the neighboring countries on a daily diet of hatred for the Jewish state. There is no proposal to prohibit the influx of such radicalized elements into the proposed ministate.

In sum, the proposition of a third state in Palestine promises to be a nightmare, not only for Jew and Arab, but for America still under the illusion of moderating from afar the inflammatory Middle East.

It is one of the fallacies of this tragic conflict that whatever its cause there must still somehow be a solution which recognizes "the legitimate rights of the Palestinians" and provides some satisfaction for the desires of "Palestinian nationalism." Such an argument overlooks the realities of security in the Middle East, both Israeli and American. One hears talk of a "Palestinian nation" as if the area were composed of differing nations each having their separate identities and independent goals. How simple the situation would be if Israel had Palestinians to its east, "Golanians" to its north and "Sinaians" to its south in the same way as France is surrounded not by Germans on all sides but by Spaniards, Dutch, and Italians, in addition to Germans, each with their separate mature identities and a clear desire to live and let live. If such were the case in the Middle East, Israel could benevolently accept statehood for the so-called displaced Palestinian Arabs. The hard truth, however, is that while the Arabs of Palestine have developed a localized identity, they are still Arabs first and Palestinians second—and this relationship of peoples in the Middle East is still far from settled and mature. As Arabs, they can make no valid claim to the establishment of a twenty-first Arab state, this one in the heartland of historic Palestine. No valid claim, that is, if there is a valid American interest in the maintenance of a secure, strong and democratic Israel as a solution to the Jewish problem. In fact, the Arabs of Palestine already possess the potential for cultural and national development within the Jordanian state of Palestine.[4]

The clearest recent example of the whirl of passions in the Middle East, destructive not only of the Arabs themselves but of American interests, is the present situation in Lebanon. The civil war waged against Christian positions and the fratricidal war between Syrian and Palestinian should be indicative as to the kind of blood bath a Palestinian state would offer the Middle East. It is astonishing to note that there are policymakers who, through a diplomacy of defeat, see any good for America in the current Syrian domination of Lebanon.

Advocates of a third Palestinian state must ponder the probable Israeli reaction to terror emanating from territory not under their control. The obvious Israeli answer would be the unauthorized "policing" of the new rump state. Given the traditional cycle of terror and reprisal, the region would be continually on the brink of war. Jordan might propose that it be permitted to police the area, but then we would no longer be talking about a third Palestinian state.

As of the time of writing, Israel has succeeded in establishing reasonable security along the Lebanese frontier largely because of the willing and active cooperation of Christian forces in that area. Such a happy circumstance exists nowhere else in the region. To ask Jerusalem to countenance another Arab state, this time in the heartland of Palestine, where terror would become endemic, is foolhardy in the extreme.

The issue of Jerusalem is the most telling reason for not promoting the establishment of a third state. If Jerusalem were excluded from the contemplated state, it would be a fulcrum for passionate irredentism, even though Muslims pray facing toward Mecca, not Jerusalem.

If, on the other hand, parts of Jerusalem were to be included, it would surely give rise to terror and retaliation within the very heart of Israel's capital. The assumption that Arab and Jew will continue to live in peace in Jerusalem after the removal of Israeli policing is ludicrous. The hard reality remains that unless Israel and Jordan can establish joint control over central Palestine, there can be no substitute for Israeli sovereignty over the area. Flippant talk about East Jerusalem as an integral part of a new state is dangerously irresponsible if one wishes to safeguard the Holy City as a place of peaceful encounter among all peoples and religions.

Further Israeli withdrawals on the Egyptian and Syrian fronts as part of a plan for the establishment of a Palestinian state would only compound Israel's insecurity. The United States should not be put into a position of being asked to guarantee such an untenable situation in which Israeli forces would be asked to move back from the front lines of Israel's defense at the very time that a new situation of uncertainty and instability is inserted into the center of the region. If indeed the mistaken belief prevails in American councils that the cause of the Arab-Israeli conflict is a denial of self-determination to the Arabs of central Palestine, then we should at least be very cautious with regard to the other borders of Israel. Otherwise, the temptation would be great on the part of the confrontation states—Syria, Egypt and Jordan—to attempt a *coup de grace* against Israel as the security situation in Palestine deteriorated. By way of tentative conclusion here, it can be said that enough time should be given to Israel and Jordan to resolve the issue of coexistence and to allow a working relationship to develop before final accommodation is reached in the Sinai and on the Golan Heights. An inability to recognize this necessity is an inherent fallacy of the global Geneva approach. It is in fact more sensible for the Arabs to be asked to rely on Israeli guarantees with respect to future withdrawals than to ask Israel to place its existence in the hands of any proposed guarantor of its security. It is not the Arab states which are threatened with "politicide"—the extinguishing of sovereignty. The very thought that the United States should have to guarantee Israel rather than Israel guaranteeing its Arab neighbors is but one more reflection of the politics of defeat under which our diplomacy has long suffered.

What would be the American response should a Middle East confrontation occur with or without Soviet intervention at the very time that the Soviets are moving militarily against independent pro-Western forces in Yugoslavia or, say, Italy? One hazards the guess that we as a nation would be so demoralized by our politics of defeat that we would lose control of the Mediterranean by default. Only a forthright policy of defending the security and potency of Israel can thwart Soviet designs in the area. The Israelis have more important things to do in the service of American strategic interests than to have to fight Arabs and at just the moment when we may need their facilities and capabilities in support of military operations elsewhere.

In conclusion, it must be clearly stated that the United States has no interest in yet another partition of Palestine and that it is in its highest security interest to press for a direct accord between Israel and Jordan for the purpose

of achieving progressive integration and cooperation between the two peoples of historic Palestine.

The true tragedy of the Palestinian terror organizations
is that they are only now coming to understand the extent
to which they are simply tools in the hands of the rival
Arab states. If Israel were to disappear tomorrow, Palestine would become a battleground for imperial domination
between Syria and Egypt, as it has so many times in the
history of that war-torn region. It is indeed important to
reflect that only a strong Israel astride the kingsway of
the Middle East can safeguard those necessary conditions
on the ground, permitting the Arabs of Palestine on both
banks of the Jordan River to maintain an independent
national existence.

X

CONCLUSION:
PEACE AND
THE SECURITY
OF THE WEST

O VER the past three decades, the overall Western
position in the Middle East has progressively eroded
from a position of paramountcy to one of deference to
rising Soviet power. When viewed in terms of the State
Department's explicit objectives, United States Middle
East policy is a failure. Far from blocking Soviet penetration, the Kremlin today makes use of a string of bases
and naval facilities in Iraq, South Yemen, Somalia, Syria
and Libya, not to mention an intimate familiarity with
the military facilities of Egypt. The armies of all these
countries are totally dependent on Soviet equipment.
What was once secure Western access to oil is today
imperiled by the designs of Arab radicals and Soviet
strategy for manipulation of the region. As for the stability

of the region and containment of local conflict one has
only to look at Lebanon.

Our futile attempts to foster an alignment of Arab
revolutionary regimes against the Soviet Union is a dismal
failure only made worse by fleeting fancies of success.
Rather than strengthening our ties with Turkey and Iran,
a highly successful Soviet policy of accommodation and
cooperation has been permitted. Our hopes for promoting
democratic structures in the Arab states have been totally
dashed as each succumbed to military rule however disguised in parliamentary forms. Our present arms policy
assures the deepening and extension of dictatorships based
solely on the will of the military.

All of these failures have been exploited by the Soviet
Union. Today the Soviet fleet has the run of the Mediterranean, free access to the Indian Ocean and is extending
operations around the globe. This assertion of Soviet
military power at both ends of the Middle East has a
wider perspective as shown in the body of this study.
Its ultimate target is the isolation and neutralization of
the United States through the dominance of Western
Europe and China. In the Soviet design, Western Europe
will fall into the Soviet sphere of influence once its oil
lifeline is controlled either at the wellhead or at its various
choke points. China can be neutralized by means of
Soviet encirclement running through the Middle East.

For three decades the Soviets have been probing the
soft flank of Europe which is the Middle East and testing
its turbulent waters for strategic gain against the United
States. There has been no effective American response to
such repeated probes. As America has attempted to assert
its role in the region it has displayed an alarming

degree of indecision and ignorance with regard to the dynamics and power relationships within the region. In the Soviet view, the United States politics of defeat in the Middle East promises a repeat of the acute American setback in Indo-China when the United States was confronted with Soviet power through third parties on the ground. We are misreading the realities of the Middle East as assuredly as we failed to grasp the indigenous forces at work in Southeast Asia.

The Soviet view goes on to conclude that its power has compelled the United States to reappraise the content and priorities of its policies: cognizant of "new realities," the United States is supposedly adjusting to the lowest limit of its capabilities. We, as a nation, have forgotten what our best effort can indeed be.

It is imperative that we renounce the supposed United States policy goal of acknowledging the Kremlin's "legitimate" or even "formal" role in the Middle East and realize that Moscow's true design is to exclude all American power from that region. The Soviets do not require direct physical control of the Middle East to achieve their designs against Western Europe and China.

The most recent National Intelligence Estimate regarding Soviet long-range strategic intentions finally acknowledges that Moscow is seeking superiority in arms.[1] This assessment is a reversal of past estimates that adjudged the Soviet objective as being limited to rough parity with the United States in strategic capabilities. The policy of detente was seen by the Kremlin as a convenient cover for Soviet subversive activity in regions like the Middle East in anticipation of the day when it would in fact have achieved military superiority. On that day Moscow would be able to pull a "Cuban missile crisis" in reverse on the United States and force *us* to back down in and out of the Middle East.

United States decline in the Middle East is now manifest in the escalation of Soviet naval power, the impending loss of Lebanon, mismanagement of the Cyprus problem, betrayal of the Kurds, appeasement of Arab economic aggression, submission to oil blackmail and the alarming alacrity with which policymakers are prepared to accept Moscow's demand for formal acknowledgment of its role in the region. Precisely what role is not defined but the implication given is that a definitive settlement of the Arab-Israeli conflict would be an acceptable means for achieving that goal. It is of no comfort for this writer to add that the determinant majority view in analyses of the Middle East and in particular, evaluation of the Soviet factor in the equation, are far from accurate. Few, if any, stand up to rigorous professional and academic standards.

Despite all the events described in the body of this study the mistaken belief that Soviet penetration into the region is the consequence of the Arab-Israeli dispute survives. The facile implication that given a settlement, American-Arab relations would necessarily improve and Soviet influence automatically decline is dangerous to United States security interests.

The theory that the Arab-Israeli conflict is the central issue in Middle Eastern politics was inherited from the British who pursued a policy of encouraging the Arabs to unite on the Palestine issue, a policy which gathered momentum in the last decade of the mandate, from 1937 to 1947.[2] The British then acted on the assumption that

the Palestine issue was the overriding and paramount
question for all Arab rulers and attempted to fashion a
regional and coherent pro-Arab policy at the expense of
the Palestinian Jews and the Zionist movement. Much to
their dismay, they learned that concessions in Palestine
alleviated none of their difficulties in Egypt and Iraq.

The sources of tension and conflict in the Middle East
are multiple, complex and generously distributed throughout the region. They also demonstrate that despite the
prolific rhetoric of pan-Arabism and "Arab socialism" the
more critical issues dividing the Arab states have nothing
to do with Israel and promise to keep the region in a
state of continuous tension. This is borne out by a quick
review of Middle Eastern events as analyzed in this study.
Overthrow of the Iraqi monarchy in 1958, breakup of
the Syrian-Egyptian merger in 1969, the subsequent abortive Arab summits of 1964–65, the civil wars in Iraq,
Sudan, Yemen, Jordan and twice in Lebanon tell another
tale. Indeed, in the 1967–73 period alone there were political upheaval in Egypt, abortive coups in Morocco and
Sudan, successful coups in Iraq, Syria, Somalia, Oman and
South Yemen, fighting on the Syro-Jordanian and Saudi-
South Yemeni frontiers—not to mention the Arab-Iranian
rivalry in the Gulf.

A fundamental misreading regarding the nature of the
political processes underway in Arab countries has led
many a policymaker astray. Concession, compromise and
appeasement merely give rise to new Arab demands.

Despite American opposition to the tripartite invasion
of Egypt in 1956, Washington failed to win its coveted
identification with the anticolonialist sentiment in the
region. On the contrary, American mismanagement of the

crisis weakened the Atlantic alliance, strengthened the anti-West "nonaligned" bloc as well as Nasser's position in the Arab world and accelerated Moscow's imperialist penetration of the entire region.[3] The British, French and Israeli move to defend their respective rights with regard to the inviolability of the Suez Canal was no blatant colonial usurpation of the rights of peoples to self-determination, but rather represented a clear understanding on the part of Western Europe that the viability and security of an international waterway must be maintained, even by force if necessary. When Nasser contemptuously nationalized the Suez Canal in violation of international agreement, the United States initiated a process meant to obfuscate the issue and avoid confrontation at all cost. Britain and France were, at that time, still morally strong enough to defend their rights and interests in the region. When they decided to do what was necessary for the maintenance of Western long-term interests, we could have at least kept our peace, rather than finding common cause with the Kremlin.

American desires for the middle position in all regional quarrels blurred the distinction between friend and foe, thereby weakening the will of friendly regimes to resist the Soviet-Egyptian threat. In attempting to fashion a comprehensive policy for the region as a whole policymakers seem unable to understand limitations of Arab unity. Indeed, the urge for Arab unity is based partly on religion, partly on a number of divergent political ideologies and partly on a yearning for a revival of the ancient glory and power of the Caliphate. The dream of uniting the Arabs from the Atlantic to the Persian Gulf cannot be reconciled with the fiercely individualistic character of the Arabs. At best, Arab states are governed by national authorities pursuing the interests of their own countries. At worst, they are run by military elites who use the apparatus of state to retain power and the hyperbole of pan-Arab and anti-Israeli ideology to shore up their legitimacy.

Due to the aforesaid distorted perceptions of the political processes in the region, the record of American policy is replete with indecision, ambivalence, poor judgment and retreat even in the face of weakness. One need recall but a few of the key decisions in the politics of defeat: persistent and inexplicable failure to demand that Arabs conclude a genuine peace, not another armistice, truce, cease-fire or nonbelligerency agreement; refusal to uphold the Tripartite Agreement of 1950, maintaining the arms balance in the Arab-Israel zone; abandonment of Britain, France and Israel in the 1957 Suez-Sinai war; manifest appeasement of Nasser and his aggression throughout the region; unwillingness to denounce Nasser's abrogation of the 1967 cease-fire agreement and the war of attrition; and failure to properly react to the Soviet-Egyptian violation of the August 1970 standstill agreement on the Suez front.

More astonishing is American behavior before, during and since the Yom Kippur War in reacting to Soviet moves. The policy was one of defeatism and retreat behind the facade of Soviet-American detente. In this context, the United States deliberately withheld war material from Israel during the war to the point of desperation and subsequently exerted enormous pressure to forestall a decisive Israeli victory.[4] In the last analysis, it was American action, not the threat of Soviet intervention, that saved Egypt from certain military calamity.

The fundamental weakness in America's diplomacy since 1973 is its failure to sustain the principles of United Nations Security Council Resolutions 242 and 338.* The former recognizes that a just and lasting peace should include the "termination of all claims or states of belligerency" and acknowledges the right of every state in the area to "live in peace within secure and recognized boundaries free from threats or acts of force." Resolution 338, concluded prior to the cease-fire (22 October 1973), "decides that, immediately and concurrently with the cease-fire, negotiations shall start between the parties concerned under appropriate auspices aimed at establishing a just and durable peace," in accordance with Resolution 242.

The juridical and political intention is overwhelmingly clear. Only as part of a comprehensive settlement is Israel required to withdraw its forces from the new cease-fire lines of today.[5] Nothing less than a full peace is required. Yet the erosion of both American-sponsored resolutions under what has been described as step-by-step diplomacy culminated in a further forced Israeli withdrawal in 1975. Such withdrawals have raised Arab expectations for even further retreats without their having to negotiate a comprehensive settlement. In short, the Arab expectation is for an eventual Israeli withdrawal to the vulnerable lines of 1967.

At the same time, Israel is supposed to recognize and negotiate with the PLO whose covenant rejects any alternative to the destruction of the Jewish state.[6] The word "peace" in Arab terminology is synonymous with a com-

---

* See appendixes.

plete Israeli withdrawal and the establishment of a Palestinian state, in exchange for a regime of nonbelligerency that excludes tangible and concrete actions. Face-to-face negotiations, normalization of relations and reconciliation have been precluded. The Israeli quest for peace is synonymous with open borders, free movement of peoples and goods, termination of economic and political boycotts and hostile propaganda and full diplomatic relations. These are dismissed by Arab leaders as premature for the present generation.

Ambiguous American support for Israel unwittingly encourages Arab governments to avoid the compelling necessity for establishing a positive peace. More dangerous is the post-1973 policy of extracting one-sided concessions in the name of "evenhandedness." At a time when American prestige and strength have declined, the tendency to blame the absence or slow progress of negotiations on Israel is bound to erode American prestige even further and feed a vicious cycle that will encourage even further deterioration of American assets in the region.[7] A weakening of Israel in the context of transitory and basically unstable arrangements would be counterproductive. In its global balancing act, America cannot afford to be preoccupied with a weakened and physically insecure Israel.

Today the consensus prevailing within the American government is for return to the worn-out prescriptions of the past. These include a renewed call for what is tantamount to an imposed settlement, based upon the vulnerable 1967 lines and another state for the Arabs of Palestine alongside Jordan—all of which is to be paid in Israeli coin. In this view, unless Israel submits, World War III is at hand. In the same breath, President Carter has been warned by these prophets of doom that he does not have the leisure of a learning period since events will not be that patient.

Clearly, the fallacy that American support for Israel's creation is the original sin supposedly motivated by the courting of Jewish votes in presidential elections is at the heart of our problem in trying to formulate constructive policy. Accordingly, the proffered solutions are the product of locked patterns of partisan thought that remain unchanged since the origins of the conflict. They must not be repeated after four tragic wars in the Middle East.

As of the time of writing, President Carter still has the opportunity to relieve American policy from the syndrome of the past and to undertake a fundamental review of this problem. Central to this reappraisal must be the irrelevance of the circumstances under which Israel emerged and the reality that it is a power of consequence closely tied to United States credibility.

No less basic is Arab rejection of this reality and their unremitting determination to reduce Israel to strategic vulnerability. The premise promoted by both the Soviets and the Arabs that Israel can be controlled by the United States is a false one. Yet it has tempted our policymakers in the past to pursue American objectives by exploiting what is actually only partial Israeli dependence on American arms.

While Israel currently relies heavily on American military assistance, such reliance would not prevent Israel from going it alone at whatever cost should her fundamental survival appear threatened. By exaggerating American leverage on Israel, a vicious cycle is maintained. The more pressure that the United States is perceived as being able to apply on Israel, the higher Arab expectations and the greater Soviet-American tensions. Indeed, perception of the American resolve to support Israel or apply pressure on her has been a continuous factor in all Arab-Israeli military confrontations.

The presumption that American resolve can lead directly to a comprehensive settlement is also in error. It ignores the built-in limits of American leverage since the pressure has been restricted by choice to Israel alone. It wrongly assumes that the Soviet capacity to undermine any settlement can be circumscribed. Finally, it betrays an ignorance of Arab perceptions and attitudes. Indeed, the recent Lebanese civil war, like other intra-Arab conflicts, testifies that Arab concepts of war and peace, hostility and accommodation are entirely different from ours. Although bound by a myriad of mutual defense treaties, federations and agreements, cruel and bloody warfare has been waged by Arab against Arab since the Second World War.

Fluctuations and upheavals, incitement and subversion are endemic. Due to a different scale of values, an entirely different meaning is ascribed to commitments and agreements. Since the inception of the Arab-Israeli conflict, Arab leaders have affixed their signature or have given sanction to more than twenty agreements and understandings, not one of which has stood the test of time. Indeed, the current Sinai II Agreement is already in the process of being eroded by Egypt both in letter and spirit. In spite of substantial and tangible Israeli concessions, Egypt has not moved away from the 30-year-old pattern of hostility and boycott.[8]

The proponents of an American-authored comprehensive settlement maintain that the Arabs are growing more impatient, that the Palestinians are desperate and that the region is a powder keg. However, there need be no explosion if Israel is strong and is so perceived by both the Arabs and the Soviets and as long as the United States does not allow itself to be stampeded into precipitous action.

Progress toward a genuine settlement can be envisaged in keeping with the following principles:

—that the United States and the Soviet Union refrain from substituting themselves for the local protagonists;

—that negotiations be the result of a determination by the parties that accommodation serves their respective national interests;

—that negotiations result in the establishment of borders that would provide Israel with a capacity to defend herself by her own means. In any case, Israel, like any other sovereign state, could accept nothing less, and we should guarantee nothing less;

—that a clear and unequivocal message be given to Arab oil producers that the United States will not tolerate any linkage of oil supply and pricing to so-called progress on the Arab-Israeli issue.

Beyond these basic elements for a solution, the issue of Palestine should be placed in its proper perspective. It is fundamental neither to the problem nor its resolution. It serves only to becloud the paramount issue of Israel's legitimacy in the region while injecting rhetoric that both sides have in abundance. The establishment of yet another Palestinian state can be achieved only at the price of endangering both Israel and Jordan, sooner or later through abetment by the Soviet Union. The only

practical solution to the problem of Palestine is for Israel
and Jordan to establish a new framework of relations and
mutual responsibilities in the context of a peace treaty.

The same diplomacy of defeat which would obfuscate
the true source of the Arab-Israeli conflict is also sealing
the fate of Christian Lebanon. Through American tolera-
tion of open military moves in Lebanon, Damascus has
achieved a new dominance in the Arab East despite the
fact that the Lebanese battlefield is within short reach
of Israel. We have lost our ability to distinguish between
friend and foe, between truly appendant pro-Western
powers and between radical totalitarian elements that
one day smile at us and graciously allow the evacuation
of our citizens from war zones and the next day connive
with the Soviets in their separate designs for dominance.
Under the debilitating influence of the United States
politics of defeat, we have lost opportunities to bolster
American security through a number of countries, each
with a mature and circumspect sense of its national place
in the region and a vested interest in stability stretching
from Israel, through a Christian Lebanon, to Turkey and
Iran. We dare not place our security in the hands of
Arab powers such as Syria and Iraq, who suffer from a
crisis of national identity, endemic sectarian instability
and social fragmentation. Such states will again and again
be drawn toward a temporary alliance of convenience
with the Soviet Union. They are frustrated revisionist
powers which thrive on the instability in the territory they
covet—Lebanon, Jordan and Arabia.

We must finally recognize, therefore, that the pillars
for stability in the region are Turkey, Iran and a secure
Israel. This array can be bolstered by the fostering of a

strongly independent Christian Lebanon. A new United States policy for the Middle East will have to be based on the corollary that no comprehensive policy for the Arab East as a whole is possible. At best we can maintain bilateral relations based on mutual economic advantage, not security. Failure to recognize this fact was the fundamental error leading to the ill-fated creation and demise of the Baghdad Pact.

Such a new policy would permit us to encourage Jordan to make its peace with Israel and resolve directly with her all outstanding issues in Palestine. It would also induce Egypt to abandon its pan-Arab ambitions in the East, thus encouraging it to rediscover its national identity and the material needs and interests of its famished multitudes. The independent existence of Qaddafi's radical desert fiefdom of Libya with all its oil wealth and sparse population almost within sight of impoverished Egypt is an anomaly. Qaddafi's long-sought goal of union with Egypt in a new Islamic Arab Republic can be achieved, but from Cairo, not Tripoli, and without the Libyan ruler. Faced with an indestructible Israel to the east, Egypt would naturally turn its gaze westward in more senses than one.

It should be clear that only in the context of an American realization of Israel as a strategic asset should Israel be asked to return the Sinai to Egyptian sovereignty. This, of course, would require appropriate arrangements for demilitarization and other agreements for the Sinai during a suitable period of transition to the new balance of Western power in the region.

It is only by totally reversing our current politics of defeat and asserting our national interests in the Middle

East in the face of Soviet designs that regional policy for Western security can be achieved. We, as Americans, must not forget that only the West has interests in the Middle East which it must defend. The Soviet Union has only opportunities for destroying these interests and very few independent interests of its own. Our policies in the Middle East will be doomed to failure until we finally acquire the attribute of steadfastness in the presence of Soviet pressure and intrigue. It should always be remembered that Moscow does not require dominance in the Middle East to maintain and nurture its political and economic system at home. America cannot say the same. The Russians are prepared to concede this, if we should consistently show the fortitude of our interests and the resolve of our will as the leader of free and democratic societies. A dynamic new policy departure in the Middle East can nurture Western Europe in its efforts to remain an open and free society of nations.

A vibrant Israel, passing the benefits of its technology to the Arab East through Jordan and Lebanon, will be one of the linchpins for peace in the region. A reversal of our present policy can show that for America, Israel is not an end in itself as some pro-Israel and anti-Israel forces would see it, but rather a means for fostering stability, peace and progress. Israel should not be viewed in the context of the problem of Palestine but rather in relation to the American strategic need for a strong asset in the region. It is only in the framework of the latter that the problem of Palestine can receive its true solution for the benefit of both her peoples—Arab and Jew.

CHAPTER
NOTES

I. Strategic Significance of the Middle East

1. U. S. Congress, The Middle East Resolution, Publication 7, 85th Congress (House Joint Resolution 117, as Amended; Adopted by the Senate, March 7, 1957) approved by the President to employ American Armed Forces in support of any Middle Eastern nation "requesting assistance against armed aggression from any country controlled by international communism." Text in *Department of State Bulletin*, v. 40 (March 23, 1959), pp. 416–418.

2. Eugene V. Rostow, "Implications of the Yom Kippur War," Joseph Godson (ed.), *Transatlantic Crisis: Europe and America in the '70s* (London: Alcove Press Ltd.), pp. 71–77.

3. Henry Brandon, "Jordan: The Forgotten Crisis," *Foreign Policy*, Spring 1973, pp. 157–170.

II. Moscow's Designs for the Region

1. "The Truman Doctrine" in J. C. Hurewitz, *Diplomacy in the Near and Middle East* (Princeton: D. Van Nostrand, 1956), Vol. II, pp. 273–75.

2. Walter Laqueur, *Communism and Nationalism in the Middle East* (New York: Praeger, 1956), p. 261.

3. See Nasser's announcement of the agreement and Israel's reaction in Hurewitz, *op. cit.*, pp. 402–405.

4. J. C. Hurewitz (ed.), "Origins of the Rivalry," *Soviet-American Rivalry in the Middle East* (New York: Praeger, 1969), p. 3.

5. "Ups and Downs in Dayan's Defense Strategy," *New Middle East*, March 1970, p. 18; S. Peters, "Israel's Survival Strategy," *The New Leader*, 13 October 1969.

6. Nadav Safran, "From Involvement to Intervention—the Soviet Union in Egypt," *New Middle East*, June 1970, pp. 14–15.

7. James Feron, "New Dangers in the Air War," *The New York Times*, 27 July 1969. *Ibid.*, "Israel: Vital Role of Air Force," 23 November 1969.

8. Interview printed in *Jerusalem Post*, 8 September 1969.

9. *The Economist* (London), 7 February 1970; *Time*, 9 February 1970.

10. Yair Evron, "From Involvement to Intervention—The Soviet Union in Egypt," *New Middle East*, June 1970, pp. 16–17.

11. *Aviation Week and Space Technology*, 18 May 1970.

12. "Soviets Deploy New Defenses," *Ibid.*, 13 July 1970, p. 15.

13. Murray Marder, "U. S. Thinks Russia Slid into a Mideast Vacuum," *Washington Post*, 12 July 1970.

14. *Russian Military Intervention—The Third Phase: Soviet-Manned SAM III's Move into Suez Canal Battle Zone* (Washington: Policy Background, Embassy of Israel, 7 July 1970).

15. L. Fletcher Prouty, "Israel's Peril: Our Military-Industrial Bubble," *The Washington Monthly*, September 1970.

16. Tom Wicker, "The Initiative That Went Wrong," *The New York Times*, 22 September 1970, p. 23.

17. "Israel Against the World," *New Republic*, 26 September 1970, p. 24.

18. Mohamed Heikal, *The Road to Ramadan* (New York: Ballantine, 1975), pp. 202–210.

19. Chaim Herzog, *The War of Atonement* (Boston: Little Brown and Co., 1975), pp. 24–25.

III. The Devolution of United States Policy

1. Smith Hempstone, "Eden, Suez and Arab Oil," *The Washington Star*, 26 December 1973.

2. John C. Campbell, *Defense in the Middle East* (New York: Praeger, 1960), p. 146.

3. Robert McClintock, "The American Landing in Lebanon," *U. S. Naval Institute Proceedings*, Vol. 88, no. 10 (October 1962).

4. Mohamed Heikal, *Al Ahram*, 22 January 1965.

5. Letter by Phillips Talbot, Assistant Secretary of State for Near East and South Asian Affairs to Senator Bourke Hickenlooper, *Congressional Record, Senate*, 30 July 1965, p. 12902. See also Philip Horton, "Our Yemen Policy: Pursuit of a Mirage," *The Reporter*, 24 October 1963, pp. 29–34.

IV. Israel and Concepts of National Security

1. Jon Kimche, *The Second Arab Awakening* (New York: Holt, Rinehart and Winston, 1970), p. 200.

2. Mercy and Serge Bromberger, *Secrets of Suez* (London: Sedgwick and Jackson, 1957), p. 16.

3. For an absorbing account read Hugh Thomas, *Suez* (New York: Harper and Row, 1967).

4. See Randolph S. Churchill and Winston S. Churchill, *The Six Day War* (Boston: Houghton Mifflin Co., 1967) and Nadav Safran, *From War to War: The Arab-Israel Confrontation, 1948–67* (New York: Pegasus, 1969).

5. Martin Van Creveld, "The Making of Security," *The Jerusalem Post Weekly*, 19 March 1974; Erwin Frenkel, "The Need to Modify Strategic Doctrine," *Ibid.*, 26 March 1974.

V. Arms and the Arabs

1. *The Sunday Globe*, 1 February 1976.

2. *The New York Times*, 1 August 1976.

3. *The Washington Post*, 2 August 1976.

4. See statement by Professor Alan Dowty before the Senate Committee on Foreign Relations, 21 September 1976.

5. Statement by Professor James R. Kurth before the Senate Committee on Foreign Relations, 21 September 1976.

6. See Clarence A. Robinson, "Israel Arms Exports Spurn Concern," *Aviation Week and Space Technology*, 13 December 1976, pp. 14–17.

VI. Egypt and Arab Quests for Dominance

1. Guy Wint and Peter Calvocressi, *Middle East Crisis* (Penguin Special, 1957), pp. 52–53; Jon Kimche, *op. cit.*, p. 102.

2. See Nasser's announcement of the agreement and Israel's reaction in J. C. Hurewitz, *Diplomacy in the Near and Middle East* (Princeton: D. Van Nostrand, 1956), Vol. II, pp. 402–405.

3. P. J. Vatikiotis, *Conflict in the Middle East* (London: George Allen & Unwin Ltd., 1971), pp. 92–99.

4. John C. Campbell, *Defense of the Middle East* (New York: Praeger, 1960), p. 146.

5. Robert McClintock, "The American Landing in Lebanon," *U. S. Naval Institute Proceedings*, Vol. 88, no. 10 (October 1962), p. 69.

6. John Bulloch, "Oil Seals the Arab Gaps," *The Daily Telegraph*, 13 September 1973.

7. Heikal, *op. cit.*, p. 16.

8. See Eugene V. Rostow, "Israel in the Evolution of American Foreign Policy," Paper delivered at the Annual Meeting of the American Historical Association, Washington, D. C., 28 December 1976.

9. Daniel Dishon, "Syria's Dilemma," *The Jerusalem Post Weekly*, 8 June 1976.

VII. Persian Gulf Rivalries in Moscow's Equation

1. Vatikiotis, *op. cit.*, pp. 99–100.

2. This is more fully discussed in my *Conflict and Tension Among the States of the Persian Gulf, Oman and South Arabia* (Air University, Maxwell AFB, Ala., 1971).

3. For an authoritative exposition see Rouhollah K. Ramazani, *The Persian Gulf: Iran's Role* (University Press of Virginia, 1972).

4. This report was leaked in 1976 by former CBS correspondent Daniel Schorr.

5. Omran Yahya Feili and Arlene R. Fromchuck, "The Kurdish Struggle for Independence," *Middle East Review*, Vol. IX, no. 1 (Fall 1976), p. 57.

6. See "Son of Secret Sellout" by William Safire, *The New York Times*, 12 February 1976; Wolf Blitzer, "The Second Betrayal," *The Jerusalem Post Magazine*, 11 February 1977.

VIII. Arab Oil and Threats to Western Security

1. Carl Solberg, "The Tyranny of Oil," *American Heritage*, December 1976, pp. 9–13, 78–83.

2. Part IV Senate Foreign Relations Committee, 30–348, January 30, 1974.

3. Parts VII and VIII 1974. Subcommittee Report, 2 January 1975. Interview with Senator Frank Church as reported in *The Washington Post*, 25 August 1974.

4. M. A. Adelman, "World Oil Market" *The Energy Question and International Failure of Policy* (University of Toronto Press, 1974), p. 18.

5. Address to Motor and Equipment Manufacturers Association Convention, Boca Raton, Florida, 3 October 1974.

6. "The Cartel's New Blow to the World Economy," *Business Week*, 10 January 1977, p. 61.

7. Heikal, *op. cit.*, pp. 276–79.

8. Collected Essays in "The Uses of Arab Oil Power," *Middle East Review*, Winter 1975/76.

9. Fred Schulman statement before Committee on Finance, United States Senate, 11 July 1975; also "Foreign Policy Influenced by Oil Companies," *Capitol Hill Forum*, May 1975.

10. "Kissinger on Oil, Food and Trade," *Business Week*, 13 January 1975, pp. 66–69, 73–74, 76.

11. *Oil Embargo Lessons and Future Impact* (H–2–35–BN 1974). A collection of papers by five Hudson Institute energy experts that make the case for an American and European policy to increase independency from Arab oil. They assert that independence is feasible within a decade. The possibility is further discussed in Fedoruk Nicholas's *Energy Crises Management: A Study of Energy Systems Command, Control and Communication* (HI–2132–RR, October 1974).

12. Fred Schulman, "The Energy Crisis—Problem or Challenge." Presented at First World Conference on Hydrogen Energy in Miami, March 1976.

13. The first comprehensive treatment for nationalization of Middle East oil industries in Soviet writings appeared in 1961: *The Near East: Oil and Independence* (Moscow 1961). The authors R. N. Andreasyan and A. Elyanov present nationalization as the prerequisite for economic and social advance in the Middle East countries. The Middle East "is not only the world's leading exporter of oil, but is also the main supplier of this valuable strategic raw material to the economic and military machine of the West European members of the aggressive North Atlantic Pact."

IX. The Problem of Palestine

1. Reference the standard works of Yehoshafat Harkabi, "Resolutions of the 13th Palestinian National Council: The Extreme Position of the PLO," *Jerusalem Post*, 29 March 1977; *Arab Attitudes Toward Israel* (New York: Hart Publishing Co., 1972); *Palestinians and Israel* (New York: John Wiley & Sons, 1974); *The Problem of the Palestinians* (Jerusalem: Israel Academic Committee on the Middle East, 1973); *The Palestinian National Covenant*, a booklet translated from three *Ma'ariv* articles (3, 17 April and 20 June 1970).

For the most recent authoritative analysis read Bernard Lewis, "Settling the Arab-Israeli Conflict," *Commentary*, Vol. 63, no. 6, June 1977, pp. 50–56.

2. See diverse collection of essays on the theme of Palestine and Palestinism, Parts I and II in *Middle East Information Series* (American Academic Association for Peace in the Middle East, Fall 1973: Winter 1973–74).

3. An exhaustive treatment by Augustus R. Norton, *Moscow and the Palestinians: A New Tool of Soviet Policy in the Middle East* (Center for Advanced International Studies, University of Miami, 1974). See also Moshe Maoz, *Soviet and Chinese Relations With the Palestinian Guerrilla Organizations* (The Leonard Davis Institute for International Relations, Hebrew University, March 1974).

4. See statement by Mordechai Abir on *The Palestinian Issue in Middle East Peace Efforts* (Hearings Before the Special Subcommittee on Investigations of the Committee on International Relations, House of Representatives, 94th Congress, 1 October 1975, pp. 73–81).

X. Conclusion: Peace and the Security of the West

1. *The New York Times*, 26 December 1976.

2. Elie Kedourie, "Quest for Stability," *Soviet-American Rivalry in the Middle East*, J. C. Hurewitz (ed.), p. 193.

3. E. Kedourie, "Suez: Expedition to an Eclipse," *The Daily Telegraph*, 30 October 1976.

4. Edward N. Luttwak and Walter Laqueur, "Kissinger and the Yom Kippur War," *Commentary*, Vol. 58, no. 3 (September 1974), pp. 33–40.

5. Eugene V. Rostow, "The United States and the Middle East," *The Middle East: Critical Choices for the United States* (Boulder, Colorado: Westview Press, 1976), pp. 47–65.

6. The Palestinian National Government formulated in 1964, revised and reissued by The Palestinian National Council in Cairo in July 1968. Its basic thesis is the destruction of the state of Israel, and the creation, in its place and in the rest of Palestine west of the river Jordan, of a "secular bi-national, democratic" state of Palestine. Key clauses are articles 2, 5, 6, 9, 19, 20, 21, and 33.

7. Former Secretary James Schlesinger's address to 17th Annual Policy Conference of the American-Israel Public Affairs Committee, 4 May 1976. *Near East Report*, 12 May 1976.

8. Although not widely known, Egypt has become increasingly remiss in fulfilling its obligations under the interim accord of September 1975. These violations include unauthorized permanent increases in the number of troops allowed in the buffer zone and the establishment of fortifications in excess of the number agreed upon. Moreover, there has been no toning down of hostile anti-Israel propaganda in the official Egyptian media, and the PLO *Voice of Palestine* radio station in Cairo has resumed its broadcasts. Egyptian activity against Israel at the UN and other international agencies and at Islamic conferences are too numerous to cite here.

BIBLIOGRAPHY

AlRoy, Gil Carl, *Behind the Middle East Conflict: The Real Impasse Between Arab and Jew* (New York: G. P. Putnam's Sons, 1975).

———, *The Kissinger Experience: American Policy in the Middle East* (New York: Horizon Press, 1975).

Carmichael, Joel, *The Shaping of the Arabs: A Study in Ethnic Identity* (New York: Macmillan, 1967).

Cohen, Aaron, *The Arab Population in the Israel-Administered West Bank and Gaza Strip* (London: Institute of Jewish Affairs, 1972).

Copeland, Miles, *The Games of Nations: The Amorality of Power Politics* (London: Weidenfeld and Nicolson, 1969).

Cottam, Richard W., "*Arab Nationalism*," *Attitudes Toward Jewish Statehood in the Arab World*, ed. Gil Carl AlRoy (New York: American Academic Association for Peace in the Middle East, 1971).

Draper, Theodore, "From 1967 to 1973: The Arab-Israeli Wars," *Commentary*, Vol. 56 (December 1973).

209

————, "Appeasement and Detente," *Commentary*, Vol. 61 (February 1976).

————, "Detente," *Commentary*, Vol. 57 (June 1974).

Elon, Amos, *The Israelis: Founders and Sons* (New York: Holt, Rinehart and Winston, 1971).

Farhi, David, *The West Bank: 1948–1971: Society and Politics in Judea and Samaria, NEW MIDDLE EAST* (November 1971).

Field, Michael, *A Hundred Million Dollars a Day: Inside the World of Middle East Money* (New York: Praeger, 1975).

Goitein, S. D., *Jews and Arabs: Their Contact Through the Ages* (New York: Schocken, 1955).

————, "Minority Self-rule and Government & Control in Islam" *Studia Islamica*, Vol. 31 (1970).

Haim, Sylvia G. (ed.), *Arab Nationalism: An Anthology* (University of California Press, 1962).

Halpern, Ben, *The Idea of the Jewish State* (Cambridge: Harvard University Press, 1969).

Harkabi, Yehoshafat, *Arab Attitudes to Israel* (New York: Hart, 1972).

Heikal, Mohamed, *The Road to Ramadon* (New York: Ballantine Books, 1975).

Herzog, Chaim, *The War of Atonement, October 1973* (Boston: Little, Brown and Company, 1975).

Hirschman, Ira, *Red Star Over Bethlehem* (New York: Simon and Schuster, 1971).

Hurewitz, J. C., ed., *Oil, The Arab-Israel Dispute, and the Industrialized World: Horizons of Crisis* (Boulder, Colorado: Westview Press, 1976).

————, *Soviet-American Rivalry in the Middle East* (New York. Praeger, 1969).

Katz, Shmuel, *Battleground: Fact and Fantasy in Palestine* (New York: Bantam, 1973).

Kedourie, Elie, *The Chatham House Version and Other Middle Eastern Studies* (London: Weidenfeld and Nicolson, 1970).

————, *England and the Middle East: The Destruction of the Ottoman Empire, 1914–1921* (London: Bowes and Bowes, 1956).

Kiernan, Thomas, *Arafat: The Man and the Myth* (New York: Norton & Co., 1976).

Kimche, Jon, *The Second Arab Awakening* (New York: Holt, Rinehart and Winston, 1970).

Laqueur, Walter, *Communism and Nationalism in the Middle East* (New York: Praeger, 1956).

Lerner, Daniel, *The Passing of Traditional Society: Modernizing the Middle East* (Glencoe: The Free Press, 1958).

Lewis, Bernard, *The Middle East and the West* (New York: Harper and Row, 1964).

————, "The Anti-Zionist Resolution," *Foreign Affairs*, October 1976.

————, "The Return of Islam," *Commentary*, Vol. 61, January 1976.

————, "Semites and Anti-Semites: Race in the Arab-Israel Conflict," *Survey*, Vol. 17 (Spring 1971).

————, Statement, Hearings Before the Subcommittee on National Security and International Operations of the Committee on Government Operations, United States Senate (March 17, 1971) (Washington: U.S. Government Printing Office, 1971).

Luttwak, Edward N. and Walter Laqueur, "Kissinger and the Yom Kippur War," *Commentary*, Vol. 58 (September 1974).

Ramazani, Rouhollah K., *The Persian Gulf: Iran's Role* (University Press of Virginia, 1972).

Rostow, Eugene V. (ed.), *The Middle East: Critical Choices for the United States* (Boulder, Colorado, Westview Press, 1966).

————, "America, Europe and the Middle East," *Commentary*, Vol. 57 (February 1974).

Safran, Nadav, *From War to War: The Arab-Israel Confrontation, 1948–1967* (New York: Pegasus, 1969).

Schiff, Zeev, *October Earthquake: Yom Kippur 1973* (Tel Aviv: University Publishing Projects, 1974).

Schmidt, Dana Adams, *Yemen: The Unknown War* (Holt, Rinehart and Winston, 1968).

Solberg, Carl, "The Tyranny of Oil," *American Heritage*, December 1976.

Stern, Fritz, "The End of the Postwar Era," *Commentary*, Vol. 57 (April 1974).

Tucker, Robert W., "Oil: The Issue of American Intervention," *Commentary* (January 1975).

———, "Israel and the United States: From Dependence to Nuclear Weapons," *Commentary* (November 1975).

Vatikiotis, P. J., *Conflict in the Middle East* (London: George Allen & Unwin, 1971).

APPENDIXES:
UNITED
NATIONS
RESOLUTIONS

APPENDIX I

Text of Security Council Resolution 242, November 22, 1967

The Security Council,

Expressing its continuing concern with the grave situation in the Middle East,

Emphasizing the inadmissibility of the acquisition of territory by war and the need to work for a just and lasting peace in which every State in the area can live in security,

Emphasizing further that all Member States in their acceptance of the Charter of the United Nations have undertaken a commitment to act in accordance with Article 2 of the Charter,

1. *Affirms* that the fulfillment of Charter principles requires the establishment of a just and lasting peace in the Middle East which should include the application of both the following principles:

    (i) Withdrawal of Israeli armed forces from territories occupied in the recent conflict;

(ii) Termination of all claims or states of belligerency and respect for and acknowledgment of the sovereignty, territorial integrity and political independence of every State in the area and their right to live in peace within secure and recognized boundaries free from threats or acts of force;

2. *Affirms further* the necessity

(a) For guaranteeing freedom of navigation through international waterways in the area;

(b) For achieving a just settlement of the refugee problem;

(c) For guaranteeing the territorial inviolability and political independence of every State in the area, through measures including the establishment of demilitarized zones;

3. *Requests* the Secretary-General to designate a Special Representative to proceed to the Middle East to establish and maintain contacts with the States concerned in order to promote agreement and assist efforts to achieve a peaceful and accepted settlement in accordance with the provisions and principles in this resolution;

4. *Requests* the Secretary-General to report to the Security Council on the progress of the efforts of the Special Representative as soon as possible.

APPENDIX II

Text of Security Council Resolution 338, October 22, 1973

1) Calls on all parties to the present fighting to cease all firing and terminate all military activity immediately, no later than 12 hours after the moment of the adoption of this decision, in the positions they now occupy;

2) Calls on the parties concerned to start immediately after the cease-fire the implementation of Security Council Resolution 242 in all of its parts;

3) Decides that immediately and concurrently with the cease-fire, negotiations start between the parties concerned under appropriate auspices aimed at establishing a just and durable peace in the Middle East.

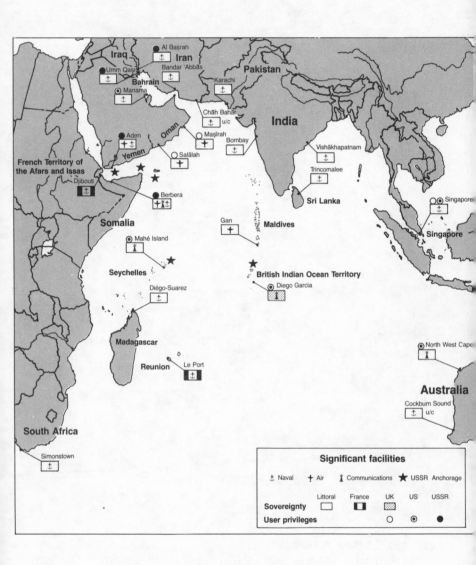

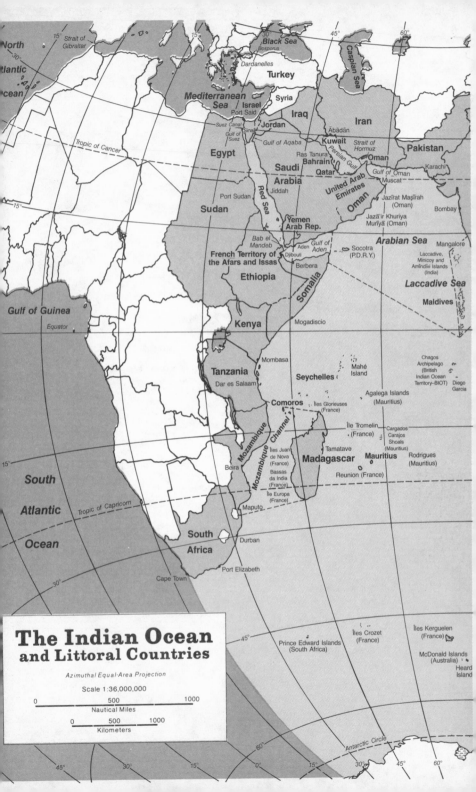

The Indian Ocean
and Littoral Countries

Azimuthal Equal-Area Projection

Scale 1:36,000,000

0	500	1000

Nautical Miles

0	500	1000

Kilometers